The Intactivist Guidebook

How to Win the Game of Intactivism and End Circumcision

Brendon Marotta

Edited by Pete Keay

Cover Design by Owen Cyclops

Published by Brendon Marotta
www.BrendonMarotta.com

ISBN: 978-1-7351134-1-8

Dedicated to those who are doing the work.

Contents

Who This Book Is For   1

Introduction   3

I. Organize   9

II. Recruit   23

III. Message   37

IV. Media   57

V. Skills   71

VI. Need   87

VII. Allies   101

VIII. Opposition   113

IX. Culture   141

X. Endgame   159

Afterward: Intact Movement   169

Appendix   177

Key Concepts   179

Glossary   181

Further Training   186

About the Author   187

Who This Book Is For

This book is for Intactivists, and those who already know circumcision is harmful.

If you don't yet understand the issue of circumcision, watch my documentary *American Circumcision*. It gives a fair overview of all sides of the debate.

Many who've seen the film have written me, asking:

"What can I do to end circumcision?"

This book answers that question.

INTRODUCTION

What Game Are You Playing?

One afternoon, I took two IQ tests.

One said I was a moron, the other a genius.

What was the difference?

The first one was timed. I didn't know that when I started. There were fifty questions and only ten minutes to answer them.

I wanted to score well, so I was double and triple checking my work – you know, like a smart person would do.

I got fifteen questions done before time was up. That meant that the other thirty-five questions were unanswered, and marked wrong by default.

It scored me at a 68 IQ.

Anything below 70 is considered mentally retarded. I don't mean "retarded" in the schoolyard bully sense. I mean it in the mental disability sense. Although offensive to some, "mentally retarded" is actually the accurate term for that score.

I hadn't realized I was being timed, so I decided to take the test again.

I calculated how much time I had for each question. At ten minutes for fifty questions, I had only twelve seconds per question. If I didn't know the answer in less than twelve seconds, I needed to guess and move on.

The questions were randomly generated, so I couldn't repeat the same answers.

Thankfully, the test was multiple choice questions. Looking at the multiple choice options, I could quickly eliminate most of them as impossible and reduce it to choosing between two answers. Many could be solved this way in under seven seconds.

The second time, I scored above 145 IQ.

Anything above 130 IQ is considered genius. I think 145 IQ is as high as the test went, since it said "above 145" rather than any specific number.

So what changed?

Did I change from retarded to genius in the span of ten minutes?

No. *I just learned what game I was playing.*

The Game Of Activism

Knowing what game you are playing can be the difference between looking retarded or like a genius.

The game of the IQ test I took was "get as many right answers as you can in under ten minutes." This is a different game than "get as many right answers as you can." If you only knew the first half of the game, you might come out looking like you had a low IQ, as I did before reading the rules.

However, many games in life do not have clearly defined rules.

The game of activism is one such game.

Many people think they know what the rules of the game of activism are. They might not be able to consciously articulate those rules, but there is an unconscious understanding of the game they are playing. However, if you were to clearly articulate each person's unconscious rules for the game of activism, you might get different contradictory answers from each person.

For example, one person might articulate the game of activism as a game of "who has the best arguments." Another might articulate it as "win elections." Does the person with the best argument always win elections? If not, these two people are playing two different games, and only the one who is playing the *real* game will win.

Other games include the game of "who is the most morally correct," the game of "who has the most accurate science," the game of "who has the most citations in academic literature," the game of "who looks the best to the public," the game of "who has the most resources and money," etc. I'm sure if I asked, you could list a dozen more games people play.

What game you play depends on your goal. For example, if you want to win elections, but you are playing the game of "who has the best argument," then if you don't win the election you can't complain "but my argument was better!" *You were playing the wrong game, and you look retarded.*

The game you play depends on what you want to win.

What do you want to win?

The Game of Intactivism

Intactivists want to end circumcision.

However, they will not win unless they are playing the right game.

In fact, even if they get the right game *halfway* right ("get as many right answers as you can"), they will lose unless they understand the *full* game ("in under ten minutes").

What is the current game Intactivists are playing?

If I was to articulate the current game Intactivists are playing, it is "share the message."

Intactivists have a clear message: Circumcision is wrong, and a human rights violation. They want to end circumcision of children. They believe the best way to win this game is to "share the message" that circumcision is bad and children should be left intact.

The question is: will that game actually lead to an end to circumcision?

If it did, I would know. Few have shared the Intactivist message more than me.

In 2018, I released *American Circumcision*, a feature-length documentary on the issue that trended on Netflix. Although Netflix does not release their data, I've been told by knowledgable filmmakers we've likely reached over a million people on the platform.

I've also done public speaking, appeared on numerous podcasts, been featured in news articles, etc. Although the film has had a dramatic impact, circumcision still continues.

If the game was just "share the message," then we should have won, right?

After the film came out, I began to wonder:

What is the real game of activism?

The Real Game

The year after my film came out on Netflix, I did a deep dive into the literature on activism, political organizing, and social change. This book is the result of that research and my attempt to answer that question, "what is the real game of activism?"

Yes, sharing the message is important, but it is only part of the game.

The goal of this book is to reveal the rest of the game of activism and *recruit* you into playing that game with me.

When I made the film *American Circumcision*, I was attempting to solve the problem: how do you "share the message" of this issue with people?

My next project solves a new problem that most aren't even aware of. This book explains that problem, and lays out a practical strategy to solve it.

However, I am not writing this book to play the game of "explain the strategy."

The strategy only works if you use it.

I'm writing to recruit you.

By the end, there will be a call to action.

I hope you'll join me.

ORGANIZE

Paths To End Circumcision

Let us suppose the end goal of Intactivism is to **end circumcision**.

If we work backwards from that goal, what are ways that circumcision could end?

Well, you could ban circumcision.

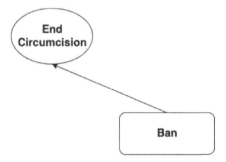

Many in the movement also believe a big **lawsuit** could end circumcision.

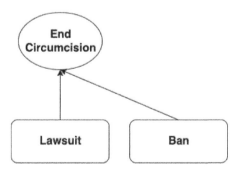

The other possibility is that you could **change culture** so much that circumcision ends, because people don't want to circumcise anymore.

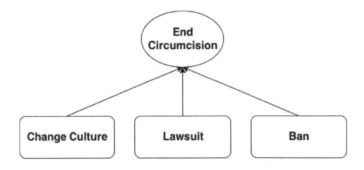

These should be fairly obvious. If you want people to stop doing something you could make it illegal (**ban**), show that it's already illegal (**lawsuit**), or you could make it so that even if it is legal, people just don't want to do it (**change culture**).

All three of those options could lead to an end to circumcision.

Some could lead to the other. For example, the news of a big lawsuit could lead to publicity that causes people to rethink circumcision and changes culture. Or, a change in culture could lead to people deciding to make laws against circumcision and banning it. However, any one of these changes alone could lead to an end to circumcision.

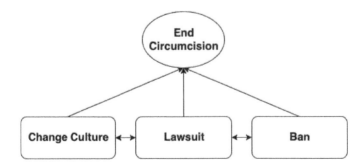

There are also several dark horse options.

For example, some have tried to convince doctors to stop offering circumcision. If circumcision was allowed, but doctors didn't do it, this would also be a win (since circumcision would not be available).

However, even in places where circumcision is not practiced, all it takes is a few persistent doctors willing to do it for this strategy to fail. In addition, it seems unlikely doctors will end a practice that is making them money.

Others have postulated that being able to heal the physical effects of circumcision through regenerative medicine would be a solution to the problem.

While this is desirable – and would likely change public perception of the issue by showing that many men do not want to be circumcised and that there is a considerable difference between having a foreskin and being circumcised – it would not end circumcision except by changing culture, which we already have listed as a potential win condition.

Many of the strategies people think might end circumcision – mass protests, lots of media, etc. – are just ways of accomplishing the conditions we've already listed (**changing culture, lawsuit, ban**).

That said, it is possible there is a way to end circumcision we are not aware of, so I'm going to include a fourth category for dark horse options – i.e. possibilities we have not considered.

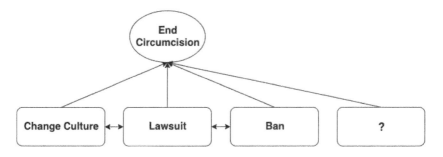

What Would It Take To Win?

So, if we continue to work backwards, what would it take to accomplish those win conditions?

First, a **lawsuit**.

What does it take to execute a big lawsuit?

Well, you need lawyers – highly skilled ones.

You can bet that if you sue doctors or medical institutions, they will have the best lawyers they can get, paid for by medical insurance. If you lose, you might have to pay their legal fees, which will be at least six figures.

So in addition to lawyers, you're going to need lots of money. Plus, you've got to pay your lawyers, which cost even more money.

You may also need additional skilled people. You might need to hire legal researchers to determine which state or jurisdiction is the right place to file your lawsuit. You might need additional researchers to find the right plaintiff or case. Once you have a case, you'll have to research the particulars of it. You might need to find and pay expert witnesses, etc.

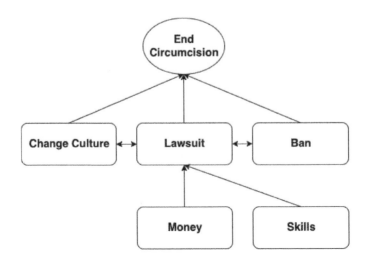

I'm going to summarize these needs as people with **skills** and **money**.

Next, what would it take to **ban circumcision**?

To ban circumcision, you would have to pass a law.

What does it take to pass a law?

To pass a law, you need a majority of votes. Depending on where you are, that could mean a majority of votes from the citizens or their representatives.

If you want to convince citizens, you'll need a lot of **people**. If you want to convince representatives, you'll need lobbyists, who are people with a particular set of **skills,** and **money** to pay them or contribute to politicians.

However, even if you have **skills** and **money**, elected officials are not likely to champion a cause they believe the majority of their constituents don't support. Even if you have **skilled** people and **money**, you'll still need a lot of **people**.

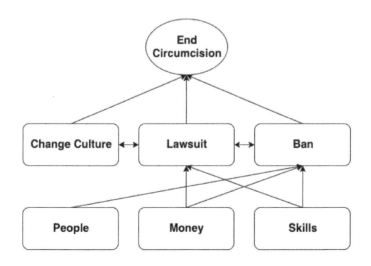

If you want to win a vote, you have to convince people to go vote for candidates who support your cause, or directly vote for the law you want them to pass. Either way – a ban will require **skills**, **money**, and **people**.

Last, what would it take to **change culture**?

Changing the culture requires persuading people.

This has been the primary focus of activists.

To reach people, you'll need **people**, obviously. There is no way to change culture without changing lots of people. You could do this one by one or on an individual basis. However, you will never reach a majority of people without a way to reach lots of people at once.

The best way to reach lots of people is media. That could mean books, movies, billboards, live events, mass protests, etc. However, all of these things require **skills** to pull off. You can't produce a film without filmmakers. You can't write scientific literature without researchers. You can't organize a protest without an organizer.

All of those things may also require **money** or resources of some kind. Even if you do not spend money on a project, you are spending people's time. The people persuading the public have to eat and pay rent. Either they are donating their time and effectively spending their own money on the cause, or someone else is covering their expenses.

Note that regardless of the strategy you have for changing public perception, at some point it will require a lot of **people**, people with **skills**, and **money** to buy those skilled people what they need, pay them, or pay for the media needed to reach masses of people.

So whatever leads to the end of circumcision, it will require **people**, **skills**, and **money**.

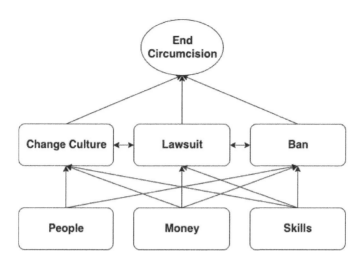

Even dark horse options will require these things. Convincing doctors will require doctors or people who can reach doctors (people with **skills**) and likely require **money**. Regenerative medicine will require researchers (**skills**) and funding (**money**).

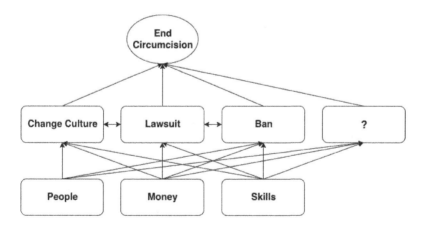

That means, if you want to end circumcision, you need to amass three things: **people**, **skills**, and **money**. Let's call those **resources**.

Just like our three ways to end circumcision could lead to each other, these three resources can lead to each other.

For example, if you have millions of **people**, and you can convince each of them to donate a few dollars, you'd also have millions of dollars (**money**). If you have millions of dollars, you can hire people with **skills** to come work for you. If you have people with **skills**, they can recruit **people**.

Regardless of the strategy you think will lead to ending circumcision, I think we can all agree: It would be easier if you had lots of **people**, **skilled** people, and a pile of **money**.

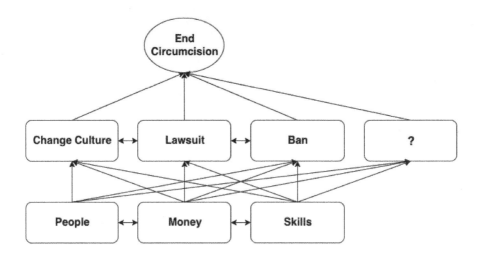

So what will lead to **people**, **skills**, and **money**?

Before we answer that, let's back up and look at what the Intactivist movement is currently doing.

The Current Intactivist Strategy

The current dominant strategy of the Intactivist movement is to "share the message."

"Share the message" takes a lot of forms – memes, protests, academic literature, media, billboards, etc. – but each form basically boils down to some variation of the strategy "we tell people our message."

There is an idea in the Intactivist movement, whether unconscious or not, that if we just tell people the message enough – loudly enough, forcefully enough, on a big enough platform – that circumcision will end, and things like a ban or change in culture will naturally flow from people accepting the message.

However, this is working from the bottom up. There is no guarantee that sharing the message will lead to change. There are many causes which the majority of the public supports that have not changed. There are also issues that have changed despite the public never being directly consulted or voting on them.

The idea that sharing the message will lead to change comes from the belief that the cause of Intactivism is so just, and circumcision such an obvious and appalling evil, that when people hear the message they will naturally change.

Experience shows the opposite. Many people retreat into denial and defensiveness when confronted with new information about circumcision. Historical just-causes were almost always met with resistance, despite most modern people now seeing them as obvious truths.

That said, sharing the message is important. You cannot get **resources (people, skills, money)** without first sharing a message that convinces someone to give you those resources. Yet the message alone does not lead to ending circumcision.

If sharing the message alone won't lead to an end to circumcision, what is the missing step?

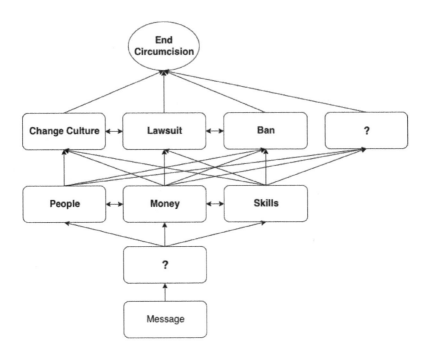

The Missing Step

Suppose you are at an Intactivist protest. Someone approaches you and says they agree with you and are against circumcision. Everyone cheers and thanks them for their support.

Then what?

Well, in the current "share the message" strategy, that's it. You shared the message; they agree; mission accomplished. They fade back into the crowd *and are never seen again*.

Did that interaction lead to more **people, skills,** or **money**?

If not, you are not any closer to the goal of ending circumcision.

The only resource you could argue you've increased is people. However, if that person isn't seen again and you have no way to contact them, they have not contributed to the goal of more people, since they are still functionally a stranger.

Compare that to the way a business functions.

If you land on a business's website, they ask for your email address. They may even offer you a free gift if you sign up for their email list, or they may try to get you to buy something and become a customer. If you do, they will re-target you with more emails and ads to convince you to buy even more of what they are selling.

A business is just trying to get **money**. Activists are trying to get **people**, **money**, and **skills**. That means they need to be three times as smart as any business, if not more.

What would happen if that activist interaction functioned like a business?

Suppose you are at an Intactivist protest again. Someone approaches you and says they agree with you and are against circumcision. You thank them and then say:

"We do a lot of events like this. I'd love to tell you about our next one. Is there an email address or phone number we could reach you at?"

Now that person is not a stranger but a person you can reach. You could contact them and ask them to show up at future events, bringing more **people**. You could ask them to contribute **money**. You could find out what they are good at and ask them to contribute **skills**.

Now, you are actually closer to ending circumcision, because you're building an **organization**.

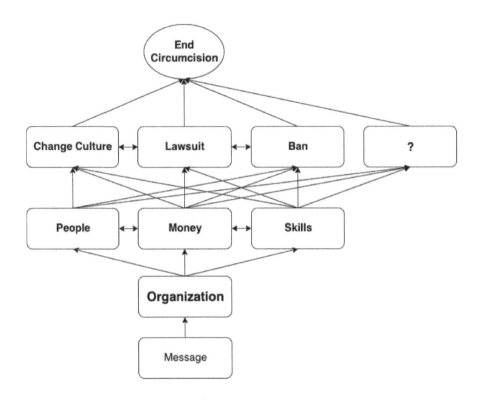

An **organization** is anything that allowed you to connect with and mobilize **resources (people, money, skills)**.

In business, you need marketing ("share the message"), but you also need a sales funnel. A sales funnel is the process by which you turn someone from a lead to a customer.

Because activists share their message, they have done a good job of creating leads, but there is no formal process of turning those leads into **resources (people, money, skills)**.

In activism, the process of turning leads into **resources** is known as **recruitment**.

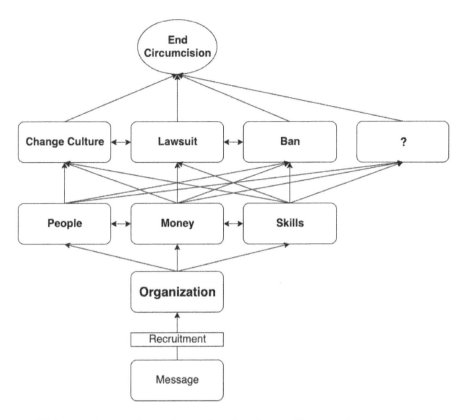

This can be made easier or harder depending on how organized you are. For example, you could add people to an email list. You could take down phone numbers by hand. You could have a website where they sign up, and you could run targeted ads for the site. You could form a legal organization and sell memberships.

Whatever you do, ***you must organize***.

RECRUIT

Do You Have An Organization?

Some of you may say, "But we already have an organization."

Yes, you might. If you have a group you can call on for **people**, **money**, and **skills**, you have an **organization**.

However, is it growing?

Many existing **organizations** are stuck at the level of "the usual suspects."

"The usual suspects" is a pattern activist groups fall into where the same "usual suspects" show up at every event, and the **organization** never grows or adds new people.

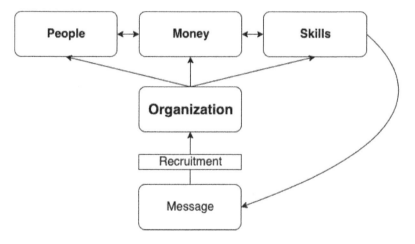

Pictured: A healthy organization in which resources spent bring in more recruits and resources.

If your organization is comprised of the same unchanging volunteers year after year, it is not a growing **organization** but a clique or social club.

Right now, Intactivist events effectively "share the message." However, if these events do not **recruit** more **resources (people, money, skills)** then they do not bring us closer to the goal of ending circumcision. They might as well be private parties.

It would only take a small change to turn a "share the message" event that costs **resources** into a **recruitment** event that gains **resources**.

The difference between wasted resources and gaining resources is recruitment.

The Intactivist movement does not yet have the **resources (people, money, skills)** to fully change culture, win a lawsuit, or ban circumcision.

This means reaching victory will require using existing **resources** to acquire more **resources**.

If your message leads to greater **recruitment**, then you will experience growth.

If your message does not lead to **recruitment**, then you will experience **burnout**.

Burnout is a feeling that comes when you spend **resources** and do not get a return on your investment.

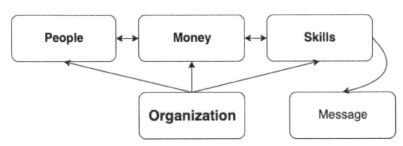

Pictured: An unhealthy organization in danger of burnout, because it is expending energy without drawing in more resources.

Why do some messages lead to **recruitment**, while others do not?

The answer lies in who you are **targeting** with your message.

The Spectrum of Allies

If you want to recruit people, where do you get them from?

On every issue, there exists a **spectrum of allies**.

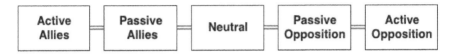

Active allies are people actively working on your cause. These are the people protesting, publishing, donating money, taking legal action, etc. Anyone who is taking action to support your cause or create change is an active ally.

Within each category there is a spectrum. For example, someone who has dedicated their life to a cause is more active an ally than someone who makes one blog post about it, or contributes a few dollars. However, they could all be called **active allies**.

Passive allies are people who support your cause but are not actively working on it. These are the people who agree with you but are not taking action.

Most people are passive allies on the issues they care about. Think about the number of issues you support. How many of these issues have you volunteered at a non-profit for, or given money to support? Even if you contribute to multiple issues, you'll prioritize some above others, since you only have so many **resources** to give.

But passive allies are still important, as they add social proof and passive support to those who are doing active work.

Neutral is where the majority of the population resides. Most people are neutral on most issues, or follow the dominant social narrative. Someone who has not thought about an issue deeply is usually neutral. Neutral can also extend to institutions. The roads are neutral. You can protest in the town square of a city because it is an explicitly neutral space, and everyone is free to share their ideas there.

Social media platforms, marketplaces, payment processors, college event spaces, etc. can all be neutral, and usually start as neutral until acted on by allies or opposition.

Passive opposition are people who disagree with you but are not working against you. Passive opposition might include people who support circumcision but have not promoted the practice, nor contributed money towards opposition groups, nor published their opinion in a place it might persuade someone else to become opposition.

Active opposition are people or groups actively working against your cause. Active opposition includes people contributing money to opposition groups, publishing pro-circumcision academic literature, running circumcision programs, creating pro-circumcision media, etc.

It should be obvious that passive and active opposition groups can be thought of as the opposite of their corresponding allied categories.

The Game Of Allies

Given this model, the game should be obvious:

The goal of active allies is to move people towards their side of the spectrum.

How is the Intactivist movement working to move people along this spectrum?

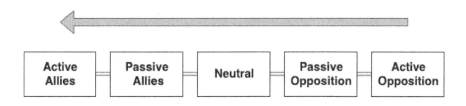

One of the primary Intactivist strategies is to ask opposition groups to stop supporting circumcision.

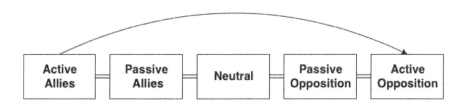

Intactivists protest the events of groups that practice circumcision. They argue with pro-circumcision users on social media. They debate strangers who approach them at events.

I believe this strategy comes from a well-intentioned place. In a healthy relationship, if you tell someone that their behavior is hurting you, they stop. It is natural to assume that if you show pro-circumcision organizations and people that their actions are harming children, they will also stop.

However, this is the *least effective strategy*.

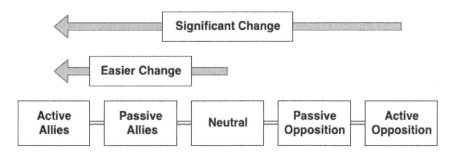

Opposition groups are the least likely to become active allies, because they have the furthest distance to move. While it is possible for someone to suddenly "see the light" and jump from one side of the spectrum to the other, the more common scenario is for people to slowly slide from one side of the spectrum to the other, one notch at a time.

The Slow Slide Of Opposition

Messaging the opposition might make them change, but only a little bit at a time.

For example, the American Academy of Pediatrics once recommended circumcision. Nowadays, their position is that they do not recommend it. They moved from actively recommending circumcision (**active opposition**) to passively supporting it (**passive opposition**).

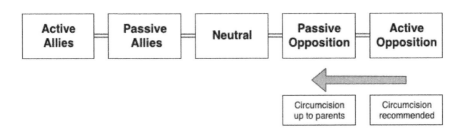

In their own view, the American Academy of Pediatrics has heavily moderated on this issue. Some in their organization see them as neutral. However, in the view of Intactivists, they are still promoting circumcision – and anything short of total condemnation of circumcision is unacceptable.

This is because the Intactivist movement sees circumcision as a human rights violation. Many compare it to rape. If we were to create the same spectrum for the issue of rape, virtually everyone in the modern world would be in the **allies** category.

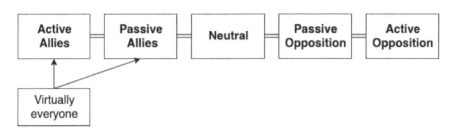

On the issue of rape, there might be a few people who are **passive allies**, meaning if they saw a rape happening they wouldn't want to get involved, but virtually everyone agrees: rape is bad.

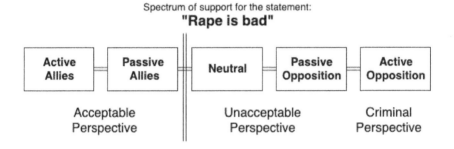

If someone was to say they were "neutral" on the issue of rape, or that they personally would never rape anyone, "but it's fine if you want to," we'd see them as a monster. On the issue of rape, any position but condemnation is unacceptable.

If circumcision is a form of rape, then the same moral framing is true. As a consequence, many Intactivists see **neutral** groups as opposition, when they are actually closer to the Intactivist position than to **active opposition**.

While it may be the case that neutrality is not a morally acceptable position, it is also true that moving from **active opposition** to **passive opposition** is an improvement. Any movement closer to **allies** is progress, even if there is further to go.

However, moving the American Academy of Pediatrics from **active opposition** to **passive opposition** took nearly *two decades*.

Was this an effective use of **resources**? Did it increase our **resources (people, money, skills)**, or has it drained them? Could those **resources** be deployed better elsewhere?

Creating Allies Is Easier

This focus on opposition ignores the greatest potential for growth: **neutral** and **passive allies**.

Moving someone from **neutral** to **allies** is a much shorter move than moving someone from **active opposition** to **active ally**, and *requires less resources*.

The amount of work and **resources (people, money, skills)** required to make someone who has "never thought about this issue" see the light is much lower than convincing **active opposition**, or even **passive opposition**, to do the same.

If you want the highest reward, focus on those closer to you.

Passive allies are the most overlooked category.

A "share the message" strategy doesn't recognize the need to mobilize people who already believe the message but have not taken action (**passive allies**).

However, if the way to end circumcision involves turning leads into **resources (people, money, skills)** by **recruiting** them to an **organization**, then only active allies actually further the cause.

I'll repeat that:

Only active allies actually further the cause.

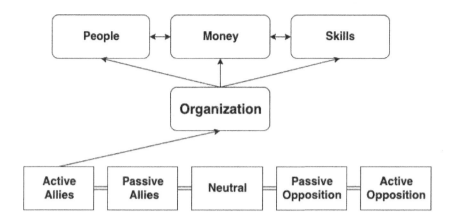

Turning a **passive ally** into an **active** one is the easiest move on the spectrum, and the most overlooked.

What would it mean if every **passive ally** started attending events, donating money, and contributing their skills? How much more could you do?

The most important shift on this spectrum is finding ways for **passive allies** to become **active allies**.

The Intactivist movement has a lot of people who agree (**passive allies**), but the movement does not give them many opportunities to become active or seek ways to recruit them beyond asking them to "share the message."

Recruit Passive Allies

Imagine you are at an Intactivist protest.

You talk to a hundred people. Only fifteen of them agree with your message.

In the "share the message" model of activism, this is a failure.

You experienced eighty-five rejections. Only fifteen people actually received the message.

This is to be expected. At the time I'm writing this, only about fifteen percent of the American population agrees with the Intactivist message, so fifteen out of a hundred is about right.

However, experiencing that much rejection can be draining, especially if you are not taking energy in. You might have been yelled at by people who disagree with you, or had extended debates with people who will never change their mind. Plus, you have no measurable way of seeing if you are any closer to the goal of ending circumcision.

Now imagine, you talk to a hundred people. Fifteen agree with you.

You collect their contact information and follow-up with them.

Five of the fifteen actually respond. One gets involved in the issue.

Maybe he contributes money. Maybe he shows up at the next event.

Now you are *actually* one person closer to ending circumcision.

Recruitment Is More Effective

In our imaginary scenario, you talked to a hundred people. What if you dropped your attention from the eighty-five that won't convert, and *solely* focused on the ones that would?

What if you didn't spend an hour debating the guy who would never change his mind? What if you didn't engage with the person who just yelled obscenities?

How much more energy and resources would you have to use for recruiting?

In fact, what if instead of doing a protest – where you encounter people of all perspectives – you did an event targeting people likely to agree with you?

This is counter-intuitive. Current Intactivist thinking would see this as a waste of time. Why would you "share the message" with people who are likely to already agree with you? Shouldn't you focus on getting people to "see the light" that circumcision is wrong?

If our goal is to end circumcision, then we need **resources** (**people, money, skills**).

Who is most likely to contribute those? **Passive allies**, **neutrals**, or **passive opposition**?

Now, imagine you hold a private event for people likely to agree with you. You speak to twenty-five people. Ten show interest. You follow up, and five decide to get involved in this issue.

If organizing is the goal, that private event for twenty-five was a greater success than your protest talking to a hundred, even though you didn't "share the message" with as many people.

Plus, if you decide to do a protest later, you will have five more people at your protest, recruited from your private event. Each of them will also be talking to people.

Suppose that at an average protest you talk to a hundred people. Your new recruits talk to an average of fifty people, because they are half as effective as an experienced activist like you.

If you just did two protests, you'd reach two hundred people. If you did a private event and protested with your new recruits, you'd reach *three hundred and fifty people*, because you'd talk to a hundred, and your five new allies would talk to two hundred and fifty.

Even if you had a straight "share the message" goal, **recruitment and organizing is the more effective strategy**.

But wait – what if you recruited more people while your new recruits protested? What if you had your five new recruits *also* start recruiting?

How big could you grow this?

Recruitment As Exponential Growth

Remember this cycle we showed earlier?

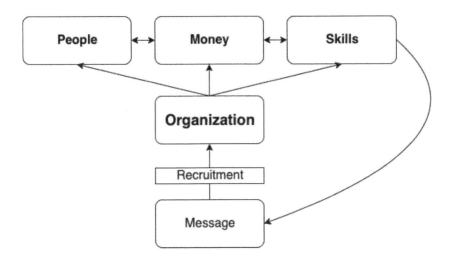

If you are actively **recruiting**, you are using your **resources** (**people, money, skills**) to grow your **resources**. Every time you "share the message" you gain more people **resources**, who share the message and **recruit** people, which brings you more people and **resources**, and so on.

This creates exponential growth.

Meanwhile, on a pure "share the message" model, you will *never* reach the **resources** needed to end circumcision (**change culture / lawsuit / ban**).

In the organizer model, we are still sharing the message – but the more complete rules we are playing by is "share the message, *and recruit people to your organization.*"

If you want your **organization** to grow, **you must recruit**.

MESSAGE

What Is The Best Message?

If the message is the "sales funnel" that brings people into **organization**, what should our message be?

More attention has been paid to this step than any other part of the Intactivist movement. Most people are unaware of the need for **organization** or **recruitment**, but in a "share the message" model, what message you share is of the utmost importance.

There is a lot of debate over messaging.

"We should be gentle, because this issue is triggering."
"We should be angry, because this issue is wrong!"
"We should be logical, because the facts are on our side."

People have had success with all of these styles of messaging.

People have also had failure with all of these styles of messaging.

What makes the message work sometimes, and not others?

Perhaps the difference isn't the message, but who you are targeting with your message.

If this is the case, then **you need different messages for different audiences**.

Who Are You Messaging?

Let's go back to our **spectrum of allies**.

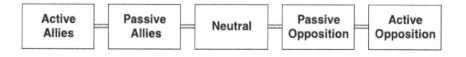

Suppose you share a message about Intactivism with people on every point of the spectrum.

Do you think they will all react the same to it?

Of course not. **Active allies** will be the most receptive to an Intactivist message, and **active opposition** the least receptive to it.

Even within each category, there will be a range of responses. You might catch someone on a bad day. You might catch someone else at the right time. Your style of messaging might fit their beliefs, attitudes, and tastes. They might associate your style with something they dislike. There are a multitude of factors.

However, not everyone responds to the same message the same way. If the best message is different for each audience, then **you need different messages for different audiences.**

Your Message Depends On Your Intention

Given that every person or group will react differently, how do you choose the best message?

The message you choose depends on your intention.

Your **intention** is what you are trying to accomplish by sharing this message.

The intention in the current Intactivist "share the message" model is almost always the same: "convince them circumcision is bad."

However, the intention "convince them circumcision is bad" usually does not work on opposition, and completely ignores passive allies, who as we've seen are the greatest growth potential for the Intactivist movement.

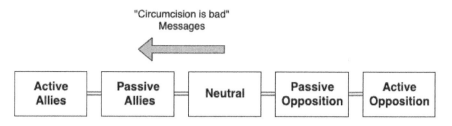

The last step of moving passive allies to active ones is critical for the Intactivist, because this is when a lead is actually **recruited** and begins contributing **resources** (**people**, **money**, **skills**).

A "circumcision is bad" message works to move some neutral audiences from neutral to passive allies.

There is of course nuance in how this message is delivered. Different styles will work better on different audiences within the category neutral. However, even the best delivery of "circumcision is bad" ignores the rest of the spectrum.

Persuading someone that "circumcision is bad" is a different thing from persuading them to become an **active ally** who is **recruited** to an **organization**. You might need to convince them "circumcision is bad" first, but the second step where they move from passively supporting the movement to contributing resources is where all the growth of an **organization** happens.

One could write an entire book on persuasion. Many have, and I encourage you to read those books.[1] However, instead of looking at persuasion, which there are already a dozen good books on, I'm going to focus on the less understood aspect: **targeting.**

Target Your Messages

Targeting is when you direct your message towards a specific audience.

---

[1] If you want to learn more about persuasion, visit my website here: https://www.brendonmarotta.com/furthertraining

Currently, Intactivists frequently target their "circumcision is bad" message towards opposition audiences. These are the least likely to accept that message.

Where you **target** depends on your **intention**. What do you want to accomplish?

If your intention is to convince an audience that does not oppose circumcision that "circumcision is bad," you need to **target neutral** audiences.

Targeting is not just about what your message is, but *where your message is placed*.

So, if the intended target for your message is **neutral** people, where are they likely to hear it?

If I stand outside a convention for doctors who practice circumcision, I'm most likely to encounter opposition. If I go to an Intactivist convention, I'll likely encounter allies. If I stand on a random street corner, I'll likely encounter a mix of people. Most will be neutral, because the majority of the public is neutral.

The same logic applies online and in media. If I publish something on an Intactivist page, it will likely reach other Intactivists or allies. If I publish something in a neutral newspaper, it will likely reach neutral audiences.

You can take the targeting further based on the category you want to target. If you want to target neutral *moms*, a parenting publication directed at women might be best. If you want to target neutral moms *about to have their first child*, a pregnancy publication might be best.

In this model, **where you share your message is as important as the message itself.**

How Poorly Targeted Messaging Happens

The idea that where you target your message matters might seem obvious, but you would be surprised how often active allies fail to consider it.

In a "share the message" model, whatever message gets shared the most is the best. Without the feedback of **recruiting**, there is also no way to track the progress of sharing the message beyond impressions.

On social media, messages are first shared with your current followers. This means the people most likely to see your message are already active and passive allies.

People share what appeals to them. What appeals to Intactivist allies is not what appeals to neutrals. If you measure the success of content by what gets shared the most, over time your content will begin to appeal primarily to allies, not neutral audiences.

This would be fine if the content were intended to target allied audiences. However, most content is made in the "share the message" model with the message "circumcision is bad" and is intended to reach neutral audiences.

What ends up happening is that Intactivists create a "circumcision is bad" message, share it with other Intactivists – who like it (because they already agree with it) – and they all assume it's good messaging without ever checking to see if it actually persuades neutral audiences.

This creates a negative feedback loop in which messages become increasingly fringe and insular as they unconsciously target other Intactivists.

Message Obscurity

Many Intactivists use insular language without realizing it.

Do you think general audiences have the same definition of "genital cutting," "human rights," or "bodily autonomy" as Intactivists do? Neutral audiences may not even know what part of the body the foreskin is.

An Intactivist motto like "the frenulum is the G-spot of male pleasure!" makes no sense to someone who lacks the sex education to know what the frenulum is, or that intact men have one. In fact, many people do not even know what the female G-spot is or where to find it. (We joke, but it's true.)

When Intactivists use terms without defining them, their messaging becomes insular. You'll notice in this book I do not assume you understand the terms I'm using. I clearly define them, and even **bold** new ones so you begin to understand my terminology.

Jargon is any word you use as shorthand for a larger concept. If I had to define the word **recruit** every time I used it and show where it fit in the organizer model, this book would be exceedingly long.

If I assumed you already knew what **recruit** meant, you might think every time you convince someone "circumcision is bad" that you've recruited them, but recruiting only happens when a lead joins an **organization** and contributes **resources** (**people, money, skills**).

See how much **jargon** that was? You understood it, because I did the groundwork to define it.

Imagine approaching an activist who had not read this book and asking them a question with those terms. They would not understand what you were talking about.

"Who are you **targeting** with your **messaging** to **recruit** to your **organization**?"
"What do you mean? I told them circumcision was bad."

There is a reason my film *American Circumcision* starts by *defining what circumcision is*. When speaking to a broad neutral audience, you cannot assume they know what you know.

Pace and Lead

How do you get an audience to understand you?

You **pace** their current beliefs to **lead** them to new ideas.

Pacing is when you say something your audience already believes is true.

Leading is when you say something your audience might not believe yet.

For example, right now you are reading this book. Your eyes can see these words, and you are really considering what this book has to say.

The first two statements are **paces**. Of course you are reading this book. You could not understand that statement if you were not. Of course you can see these words.

The third statement is a **lead**. You might not be considering what this book has to say. You could be speed reading, dismissing my words, or arguing with me in your own head. However, it's not a big lead, so most readers will accept it.

Now imagine you read: "Right now you are reading this book. Your eyes can see these words. That is because we actually live in a computer simulation ruled by reptilian aliens, who placed this book into your reality for their own amusement."

The first two statements were **paces**, but the third is a *big* **lead**. Most readers would not follow such a big **lead** and would be confused as to why the writer took them from obvious truths to such a bizarre statement.

If someone started with a **lead** that huge – "we're in a simulation ruled by reptilian aliens!" – they would sound like a crazy person and lose most of their audience.

If you identify your **targets'** current beliefs you can **pace** them and **lead** them to the idea or **organization** you are **recruiting** them into.

Leading Big

How do you **pace** someone into a big **lead**?

Let's use the statement "we're in a simulation ruled by reptilian aliens" as an example, since for most people that is a massive **lead** they would not already agree with.

Here is how you might do that:

Right now, you are reading this book. (**pace**)
It might feel and look solid. (**pace**)
However, we know from science that it is actually made up of millions of tiny atoms. (**pace**, if they know science)
Those atoms are arranged in different ways in each object. (**pace**, if they know science)
If we think of the placement of those atoms as data, then couldn't reality be understood as a collection of data, or a simulation? (**lead**)

In one paragraph, we **paced** into the idea of a simulation. That's a big philosophical concept. You might not be convinced in one paragraph, but you are at least following the logic and it sounds less crazy.

But what about the rest of our "reptilian aliens" statement?

Part of what makes "we're in a simulation ruled by reptilian aliens" such a big lead is that it's actually *three* leads packed into one. If we were to break down that statement into individual pieces, it might look something like this:

1) Reality is a simulation
2) There are these things called reptilian aliens
3) They run the simulation

Just making the first statement sound plausible took a paragraph. Each new concept requires further pacing. Those next two leads are so big they might require an entire book. However, that example sentence packs all three **leads** into *eight words*, which is why it sounds crazy.

When Intactivists say "circumcision is a human rights violation," they are making just as big a **lead** to some audiences.

"Circumcision is a human rights violation" also contains three concepts:

1) Circumcision
2) Human Rights
3) The first concept goes against the second concept

How well does your audience understand each concept?

For people who think circumcision is just a "little snip" or do not realize it removes part of the body, even calling circumcision "surgery" might be a **lead**, let alone calling it "mutilation."

You might actually have to **pace** and **lead** a less informed audience into an accurate definition of circumcision.

Some people refer to circumcision as a "little snip." (**pace**)
The cultural image of circumcision might be that it is harmless.
(**pace**)
However, our culture has been wrong about things before. (**pace** for most people)

People who've seen a circumcision describe it much differently...
(**lead**)

Likewise, how well does your audience understand the concept of human rights?

Human rights is an advanced term. Just because someone nods when you use that term does not mean their understanding is the same as yours. Most audiences do not have the deep understanding of human rights that activists do.

When someone says "healthcare is a human right," or "parents have the right to make decisions about their children," or "people have the right to choose who they associate with" they are using the term "right" differently in each example.

If you do not define your terms, when you say:

"Circumcision is a human rights violation,"

The other person might hear:

"A little snip is a genocide."

It would be reasonable to respond to "a little snip is a genocide" by asking why someone is making such a big deal out of something so small. Intactivists lament people's lack of compassion when they respond this way, but it's possible that many audiences don't even understand what activists are telling them.

Intactivist Jargon

The statement "circumcision is a human rights violation" might be better translated:

"Holding down infants and cutting off parts of their body takes away their ability to make their own choices about their body, which every human being deserves to have."

However, that's a lot more words.

Jargon is useful because it allows us to communicate complex concepts. But when activists communicate using only jargon, it becomes harder for general audiences to understand them.

A simpler concept general audiences might understand would be:

"Circumcision harms babies."

For most people, "harm" and "babies" are easily understood concepts. The idea that harming babies is bad is already an accepted **pace** for most audiences. "Violates human rights" is a more complex concept. For a general audience, "harms babies" is clearer, despite "violates human rights" containing a more complex meaning.

However, if you're writing for an academic audience familiar with human rights law, "violates human rights" might be the right phrase to use, since "harm" is not a clearly defined academic concept, but human rights is.

You can use complex concepts. You just have to define them and make them clear to your audience. Words like foreskin, trauma, ethics, etc. might all have a unique meaning among activists that has to be communicated to a general audience.

Know Your Audience

Once, I was speaking to a religious person about circumcision and said, "people have the right to their own body." He interrupted and said, "people don't have the right to their body. *God* owns your body."

For most of the Western world, the idea of bodily autonomy is a **pace**. However, for this deeply religious person, it was actually a **lead**. He did not accept the belief of bodily autonomy, so I could not rely on it as a **pace**.

You cannot assume your audience shares your beliefs.

When activists make arguments that assume others share their beliefs, they alienate audiences who do not actually share those beliefs. This is why it is important to **target** your **message** and **pace** your audience.

The best way to find out someone's beliefs is to *listen*.

Effective activists are good listeners. If you want to get better at persuading people, get better at listening. Even this book, which is a one-way monologue, includes passages that show I have been listening to the challenges of the Intactivist movement.

Ineffective activists often steamroll people, and pile **lead** after **lead** onto the conversation, without ever asking what their intended **target** already believes.

Messaging for Neutrals

My film *American Circumcision* is targeted towards the middle of the spectrum.

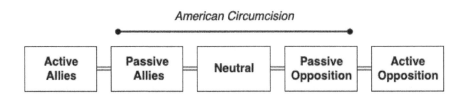

When I was testing the film, some active allies said I should call the film *American Mutilation* because "circumcision is genital mutilation." They told me I should make the film angrier, include lots of blood in the opening scene, and "really shove it in people's faces."

Would a neutral audience understand that title? Would that film appeal to them?

Here is the audience for *American Mutilation*:

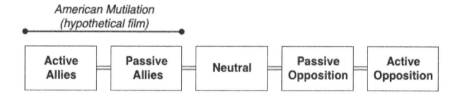

American Mutilation is a film pitch that only appeals to people who already believe circumcision is genital mutilation.

That said, I am 100% sure I could have raised money for a film called *American Mutilation*, because active allies are the ones who contribute money. I might have even gotten the same amount of praise and support from active allies.

However, this would have been a waste, since *American Mutilation* would have not appealed to neutrals and would not have helped recruit or organize existing allies, unless the message was specifically targeted for that.

As a consequence, some active allies don't like the film, because *the film wasn't for them*.

On one level, I get it. People like films targeted towards them. When I watch films on my own time, I watch things that will appeal to me. However, when making content intended to reach an audience, you have to take the needs of that audience into account.

This goes back to **intention**. What are you trying to accomplish?

The intention of my film was to take someone from ignorant (**neutral**) to informed in under two hours. That meant it needed to appeal to **neutral** audiences. The term neutral audiences use for male genital cutting is "circumcision," not "genital mutilation."

Targeting for Allies

If the intention of *American Circumcision* was to **target allies**, then *American Mutilation* might have been the right title. However, **targeting allies** would change the message.

The message of *American Circumcision* was that circumcision is an important issue.

For allies, the message "circumcision is an important issue" is a **pace**. A film called *American Mutilation* could start with that message, skip most of the material in *American Circumcision*, and start **leading** people to a different message, such as "you should contribute **resources** towards ending circumcision."

You can make messages targeted towards allies. This book is targeted towards allies.

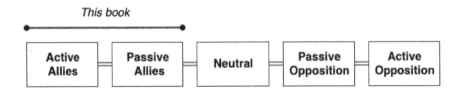

In this book, I make no attempt to explain why circumcision is bad. I assume you as the audience already agree with that message.

If you're not convinced of that or are neutral on the issue of circumcision, you should watch my film *American Circumcision*. That film is neutral. This book is not.

My **intention** with this book is to **recruit** you from being **messengers** to **organizers**.

In a "share the message" model, this book is completely useless and "preaching to the choir."

In an organizer model, this book is moving **passive allies** to **active allies**, and getting existing allies to begin **recruiting**, *which is the only thing that will actually end circumcision.*

Messaging **allies** is not about telling them why circumcision is bad. Allies already agree with you. It is about **recruiting** them to contribute **resources** towards ending circumcision. Every time you ask for donations or invite people to your event, you are messaging allies.

"We want to end circumcision (**pace**), so here is why you should contribute **resources** to my **organization** to do that." (**lead**)

Many organizations fail to **recruit resources** because they only "share the message" that "circumcision is bad." That message takes **neutral** audiences to **passive allies**. To take **passive allies** to **active allies,** you have to convince them to contribute resources.

Messaging for Allies

To convince **passive allies** to contribute, you have to convince them that this issue is important enough that they should contribute **resources**, and that your **organization** or strategy will actually help end circumcision.

Often, activists are unable to **recruit resources** because they are only focused on the first part (this issue is important), but not the second (my **organization** or strategy will help).

Suppose an activist is raising money to hire people to shout "circumcision is bad" in empty national parks across the country. Would you contribute? Probably not.

"But circumcision is really bad!" the activist protests. Yes, but that's not the issue. Shouting in empty parks is a bad strategy for ending circumcision.

This is an obviously bad strategy, but unless you communicate how the work your **organization** does is effective, it might appear just as ineffective to your allies as this obviously bad strategy does.

When I was raising money for my film, some activists said, "Why would we need a film? We already have YouTube videos."

To me, there is an obvious difference between a professionally made feature-length documentary and YouTube videos. However, you cannot assume your audience knows what you know. It would be reasonable for people to ask why I need the budget of a film for a YouTube video, if they don't understand the difference between those two things.

Since my audience did not have the same knowledge of filmmaking I did, I had to **pace** and **lead** them into an understanding of what my film would be.

Likewise, your audience may not have the same knowledge of activism that you do. If you run an **organization**, you may need to explain to your audience what you do, how it helps, and why they should contribute **resources,** by using language they understand to **pace** their current beliefs.

You'll notice that in this book I don't say you should use the organizer model because "circumcision is bad." I show how the organizer model is the only way we will ever actually end circumcision – and that **organization** is required for any other strategy you might have.

Every time you start a new project, you are messaging allies. This could be as simple as calling a friend and asking for help. It could be as big as messaging a million people to raise money for a massive campaign. Either way, the process is the same.

Neutral To Recruit

There are some **organizations** that do not reach **neutral** audiences, but are very good at **recruiting allies** to their method of Intactivism. Likewise, there are some **organizations** that reach **neutral** audiences, but do not do as good a job explaining what they do to **allies**.

The most effective **organizations** do both.

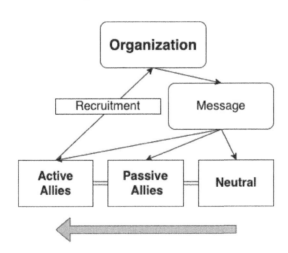

Pictured: An ideal organization that brings people from neutral to recruit.

Organizations that only target **allies** become insular, fight over a limited pool of resources, and only attract "the usual suspects."

Organizations that only target **neutrals** shift popular opinion, but suffer from **burnout**, because they never grow or take in **resources**.

Organizations that move people all the way along the spectrum are the most successful, because they can always get more **resources**.

There is a limit to the amount of **resources** currently available for this issue. **Active allies** do not yet have enough resources to end circumcision.

However, there is an unlimited amount of **resources** in the world. If you can take someone from **neutral** to contributing **resources**, you can always get more **resources**.

Bringing someone from **neutral** into an **organization** requires different messaging at each stage.

Neutral to **passive ally**: "Circumcision is bad."

Passive ally to **active ally**: "You should help us end circumcision."

Active ally to **recruit**: "Here is how you can help."

Distribute Your Message

When I screened an early edit of the film for Intactivist audiences, some activists told me that the film would not work because "we've said those arguments before."

It's true; many people in the film say things that Intactivists have been saying for a long time, but **do neutral audiences know those arguments?**

In the opening of the film, there is a moment where an older man asks an activist if circumcision removes tissue. This man has made it all the way to his elder years without ever learning what circumcision is.

Do you think he has heard Intactivist arguments before?

Were those arguments not effective, or did they just never reach people like him?

The issue with Intactivist messages is not always the message itself, but the **distribution**.

Distribution is where and how you share your message.

If you gave the best message in the world to a room of twenty-five people, the best possible outcome is that you'd **recruit** twenty-five people. That's a 100% conversion rate.

If you gave a weaker message with a 5% conversion rate to a room of a thousand people, you'd **recruit** fifty people.

Which is better? Your 100% conversion rate message might be a better message, but your 5% conversion message actually produced better results because it had greater **distribution**.

At some point, you can only fit so many people in a room. Here, your limitation is not the **message**. It's the **distribution**.

The way you **distribute** your **message** to a larger audience is **media**.

MEDIA

Media Is How You Increase Distribution

As I write, there are people watching my film *American Circumcision* who I will never meet.

I'm sitting at home, alone in my office, but my message is reaching people, because I put my **message** into **media** and **distributed** it on **platforms** where neutral audiences pay attention.

Media is messaging that reaches people even when you are not personally delivering the message.

Platforms are places where you **distribute** the **message.**

The impact of **media** depends on three things:

1) How good is your **message**?
2) How big a **platform** are you **distributing** on?
3) How well **targeted** is your audience?

I put a lot of thought into the message in *American Circumcision*, but the **distribution** is as big a part of the film's impact.

If the film were only available on my website, it would only reach my current audience. As I write, it's on Amazon, iTunes, and Netflix. Netflix is approaching a 150 million subscribers. Even if only 1% of Netflix's audience sees the film, that's over a million people.

The Netflix algorithm is designed to **target** audiences with films they are interested in. Everyone who sees the film *American Circumcision* made a choice to click on it and watch it. This means the film is **targeting** people who want to see the film.

If I stood on a busy street corner and shared a message that had a 100% conversion rate, I could not reach as many people as a film distributed to an audience of over 100 million with a lesser conversion rate.

If you want to increase your distribution, you must create media.

Current Distribution

Currently, the primary **distribution** methods of the Intactivist movement are live events – protests, baby fairs, etc. – and social media.

There is a limit to the reach of live events. You can only fit so many people into a physical space.

However, Intactivists intuitively understand the **distribution** of live events. When you hold a protest, you don't stand in the middle of the woods. You choose a busy street corner or town square as your **platform**, because these locations have greater **distribution**.

Activists also leverage their protests by sharing them on social media. By filming, photographing, and live-streaming events, Intactivists turn them into **media**, which has a greater reach.

Sometimes activists **target** existing media with their message. When Intactivists are featured in media, they rightfully celebrate. However, they are less often the *creators* of media.

Plus, the media Intactivists are featured in are usually **neutral** publications – or even **passive opposition** publications where the editors and writers clearly support circumcision. These publications are not **targeted**, and therefore have a low **recruitment** rate.

When people do create **media**, it usually has low **distribution**. They share it with a few social media followers or subscribers, who are mostly already allies. Besides, they share a "circumcision is bad" message, which is not **targeted** to that audience.

Create Media

If Intactivists wish to reach larger audiences, they must **create more media** and **distribute media on platforms that target audiences**.

Creating media requires **skill**. **Media** is produced in a *medium* – video, writing, public speaking, etc. Not everyone has these **skills**.

Part of the reason there is less Intactivist media is that activists are coming from a "share the message" model, rather than an **organizer** model.

To produce **media**, you have to **organize** people with **skills**. If activists do not organize, the only **media** created is **media** made by highly motivated **lone operators** i.e. people capable of taking a project from start to finish entirely on their own.

There are a few people capable of doing this, however an **organization** of **people** with **skills** creating **media** could out-produce all of them. Even those capable of creating solo as **lone operators** would benefit from the collaboration of **organization**.

Even from a "share the message" model, **organization** is more effective, because **organizations** can create **media**.

Media As An Investment

Media requires **resources** (**people**, **money**, **skills**). You might have to pay more up front for **media**. However, over time, it will pay back more. Once you have a piece of **media**, it will share your message even when you are not directly working on it.

Media is an investment.

Putting money into financial investments requires more **resources** up front than just working a job where you trade your time for an hourly wage. Initially, your investment may not make much. However, with enough compound interest, your investment could lead to greater wealth than an hourly wage.

Likewise, when you "share the message" with a group of people, you are trading your *time for messaging*. There is a limit to how much time and energy you can spend.

The reason activists experience **burnout** is because they spend beyond their **resources**. These resources could be **resources** as we define them (**people**, **money**, **skills**), but it could also be the activist's emotional resources and energy.

Burnout is a sort of activist bankruptcy. The solution to **burnout** is to focus on increasing your **resources** (**people**, **money**, **skills**), emotional health, or personal energy levels.

Some people are more "high energy" than others. Some gain energy from doing activism. However, there is no amount of "share the message" activism that can outperform an **organization** creating **media**.

"Sharing the message" with a group of people requires one person talking. Creating **media** requires **resources**. It might require a group of **people**, specialized equipment like cameras or computers that cost **money**, or **skills** in writing, web design, filmmaking, etc.

Those resources will pay off more because your **media** will passively share the message, even when you are not directly working on it. Instead of trading time for messaging, you are trading **resources** for a *media asset* that will continually share the message.

Media investments are not a guarantee.

If you make a bad investment, you can lose your money. Likewise, if you make bad **media** or fail to secure proper **distribution** for it, your **resources** could be wasted. However, if you don't invest in **media**, the reach of your messaging will never increase.

The solution investors use to solve the uncertainty of their investments is diversification. Most investors do not put all their money into one investment. They invest in multiple assets. If one goes down, it's okay, because the majority will gain interest over time.

Likewise, the solution to the uncertainty of **media** investments is to **make lots of media**.

You cannot know ahead of time which messages will convert.

Companies that produce **media** professionally invest millions into big projects that totally flop, and sometimes have surprise hits no one realized would succeed. If they can't predict what works, you might not be able to either.

Most movie studios, streaming networks, and publishers are kept in business by a few hits. If you make ten pieces of **media**, it's okay if nine are duds – as long as the tenth one brings in enough **resources** to cover the cost of eleven.

If you make lots of **media**, you only need to have one piece with a **message** that converts, gets good **distribution**, or is well-**targeted** in order to make your **organization** grow.

You might not be sure where to invest, but you can be certain of one thing:

Media is the most effective way to share your message at scale.

Targeting Media Platforms

There are only a few pieces of Intactivist-related media that have wide **distribution**. My film is one of them.

Given that the **distribution** is as important as the **message**, what can Intactivists do to increase their reach?

To reach larger media **platforms** you have to:

1) **Target an existing media platforms, or**
2) **Build your own media platform**

Targeting an existing media platform is when you share your message on an existing platform. Examples of this would be going on someone else's podcast, writing an article for a newspaper, giving a recorded talk at an existing conference, etc.

Building your own media platform is when you create your own space and audience to share the message. Examples of this would be starting a podcast, writing a book that you publish yourself, holding a conference or event where you record the talks, etc.

If you want to **target** an existing media platform, you have to understand them as an audience. For example, Netflix only takes certain content. To get my film on Netflix, I had to understand their needs as a **platform** and make sure my film fit those requirements.

I can put my film on Netflix because Netflix is an **organization** of **people** with **skills** that already did most of the work for me. They have employees with skills in marketing, programming, advertising, acquisition, accounting, managing people, etc. I could never do all the jobs at Netflix on my own. Because of their **organization**, I only have to contribute my one **skill** – making a movie – and they handle the rest.

The disadvantage of using existing platforms is **gatekeepers**.

Gatekeepers are people or things who determine if you have access to an **organization's resources** or not.

Some **organizations** are friendly to the Intactivist cause. Some are not. When I was distributing my film, some activists feared we would not get access to larger **platforms** because the people curating those **platforms** might not like the film's message.

It is entirely possible that an **opposition** employee acting as a **gatekeeper** for an **organization** might refuse to give my film a **platform**. There are media platforms that have refused to interview me or share my message.

The cost of using someone else's **platform** is that you have to go through their **gatekeepers**. **Gatekeepers** are like any other audience. You have to **target** them with a **message** that will fulfill your **intention**. Streaming networks, radio shows, podcasts, newspapers, academic journals etc. all have certain editorial standards. If you want access to their platform, it is your job to understand their needs and **target** them with the right **message**.

If you "share the message," but your **message** is not targeted for the **platform** you are trying to reach, **gatekeepers** will block you. If I made a bad film that did not meet Netflix's requirements, they would not have allowed me on their **platform**.

Media platforms are run by people. Some are reasonable. Some are ideologically opposed. **Platforms** run by **active opposition** might block you no matter how good your **media** or message is. That might be unfair, but it is the game.

Building Media Platforms

The other option for activist media creators is to **build your own platform.**

My film is on major platforms, but I also have a blog. Any time I want, I can go online and publish whatever I want on my blog. There is no **gatekeeper**, because I am the **owner**.

You only own media where you are the gatekeeper.

My blog does not have a significant reach. If I wanted greater reach, I would have to either 1) write for someone else's publication or 2) build up the readership on my blog.

The advantage of building a media platform is that you own it.

This disadvantage is that you have to build your audience yourself.

If I wanted to build my blog from its current state to a high traffic publication, that would be possible. There are people who have built highly influential one-person blogs.

Meanwhile, it would be less work for me to just write one article for someone else's publication which has already done the work to build an audience.

There are trade-offs with each strategy. One offers more work, but greater control. The other offers less work, but less control.

However, there is a third option:

You could build a **media organization**.

Building Media Organizations

Most big publications are **organizations**.

Big media companies do not have one writer. They have many. This allows them to publish multiple pieces of content each day, at a far greater volume than an individual writer could create.

Right now, most Intactivist media creators are **lone operators**.

A **lone operator** is a person working alone, without the benefit of **organization**.

The advantage of being a **lone operator** is that you can publish whatever you want, without **gatekeepers**. The disadvantage is that you do not have the added **resources** of **organization**.

However, **gatekeepers** are not bad if they are ideologically aligned.

I think activists are afraid of **gatekeepers** because in the past they have often been **opposition** who do not understand the issue. Trying to convince **active opposition** to become an **active ally** is a large move and expense of **resources**.

However, if the **gatekeepers** were **active allies,** publishing good content with them would be easy and not require the pain that often comes with engaging **opposition media**.

Imagine if six **lone operator** media creators came together and decided that, instead of publishing on their individual blogs and pages, they were all going to publish on the same page as a **media organization**.

Even if their output was weak, their combined **organization** would outpace any other **lone operator** media creator who wasn't six times as good as each of them individually.

Of course, creating **media organizations** requires an **organizer**.

Someone has to identify their **skills** as individual creators, **recruit** them, and align them in a common **organization**. This is difficult if each are coming from a "share the message" model and do not understand the benefits of **organization**.

Free Social Media Platforms

When I talk about the need for **media organizations**, activists coming from a "share the message" model are often confused. "What do you mean?" they say. "I can already publish what I want on social media."

First, you don't own the **platform**. Although the gate is open, that does not mean there is not a **gatekeeper**. At any point, these platforms can kill your **distribution**. Activists can and do get banned.

This doesn't mean you shouldn't use them. However, using social media is not the same as having a **media organization** that you own. Social media is a place to **distribute media**, not the **organization** itself.

Second, most activists use social media from a "share the message" model.

Sure, social media might let you share your message, but are you **targeting** new leads or just your friends list? Is your **messaging** leading to **recruitment**? Are you taking in more **resources**, or just delivering clicks to the **platform**?

Just because you are using a free **platform** does not mean the principles of **messaging, targeting, recruiting organizing**, etc. do not apply.

If anything, they apply *more*.

Most social media **platforms** are designed to get you to spend more time on the **platform**, so advertisers can sell you stuff. But activists want people to become active allies and take action.

That means if you want your **message** to lead to **recruitment,** then you have to be even smarter about how you use it, because the **platform**'s interests are aligned with consumption, not action.

Everyone Is A Gatekeeper

Every follower is the **gatekeeper** of themselves. They control where they spend their attention.

If you are building a **media organization**, you have to convince each new audience member to give you their **attention** in order to share your **message**.

The advantage of existing **platforms** is that they have already done that for you. People who follow a particular publication, show, or podcast do so because that platform has earned their attention.

If a trusted friend introduces you to someone new, you will likely trust this new person because he comes recommended to you by your friend. Likewise, if you appear on someone else's **platform**, their audience will be open to hear what you have to say because they already trust that platform.

This is true even within organizations. I would bet most of the Intactivist groups you follow, you heard about through another Intactivist. Even if you just encountered someone scrolling your social media feed, their post had to be interesting enough to make you stop.

No matter what you do, you will have to pass gatekeepers.

Use All Platforms

So should you use someone else's **platform** or build your own?

Both.

If you can get something on someone else's **platform**, do it.

If you can build your own **platform**, do it.

These are not contradictory strategies. In fact, they are complimentary.

Most people who have their own **platform** collaborate regularly and expand their **platform** by appearing on others' **platforms**.

Most people who become famous through someone else's **platform** eventually create their own.

If you have a **platform** and want to grow, appear on a bigger **platform**.

If you are on someone else's **platform** and want the freedom to speak directly to your audience, build you own.

The Limits Of Media

Media is the most effective way to get the **message** out.

However, the **message** is only step one.

Messaging does not get us closer to ending circumcision unless it leads to **recruitment**, **organization**, and **resources** (**people, money, skills**).

Don't get me wrong – **media** is great. I love **media**. I chose it as a career.

Yet **media** alone will not end circumcision.

You must **recruit**.

Let's say you do.

You have an **organization.**

You receive **resources (people, money, skills).**

Now what?

SKILLS

How Do You Deploy The Skills You Acquire?

I had a friend tell me he could only contribute one day a week to the Intactivist cause and asked my followers what he should do. The results were disappointing.

"Hold a sign and protest!" "Pass out info cards!" "Tell your friends!"

These are all "share the message" strategies. They are also strategies that require minimal **organization**. Unless they lead to more **resources** (**people**, **money**, and **skills**), this will not end circumcision.

My friend is highly **skilled**. He is one of the best content creators and social media marketers I know. He is also a standup comic. He's organized business events. His time goes for a significant hourly rate. He could contribute in far more ways than holding a sign.

However, the ways he would contribute require **organization**.

For a **lone operator** with no **skills**, holding a sign might be the best option. However, my friend has **skills** and is asking to join in a more meaningful way.

Finding a place for someone with **skills** – which we've established is needed to end circumcision – requires a structure that will allow them to best use those skills.

Multiplying Skills Through Skill Stacks

My friend has a talent for standup comedy. He wants to work on this issue. An obvious use of his skills would be to develop a short comedy routine around it.

That in itself might "share the message" better and further than holding a sign, because my friend has **skill**.

If he creates this comedy routine as a **lone operator**, the furthest reach he has is a live event like a comedy club. My friend is not famous, so there will likely only be one single room full of people who hear his routine.

However, if someone films his routine and posts it online, they could turn it into **media,** and it would reach significantly more people.

My friend cannot do standup and film himself at the same time. If he hands his cell phone to a friend to film, the audio will be unintelligible in a noisy club. To record his routine, he will need a camera person with their own gear and a lav mic to get good sound. In other words, to create **media** we need a *second person* with **skill**.

The **organization** required to get two people together for a project like this is not high. My friend probably knows someone he can ask to film. (However, a good camera person might charge **money**.)

The two of them together will reach more people than they could individually. The camera person doesn't have the **skill** of standup comedy, and my friend doesn't have the **skill** of filmmaking or his own gear. Together they form a **skill stack** that is greater than the sum of its individual parts.

A **skill stack** is a series of **skills** that are good in isolation but multiply exponentially when used together.

Right now we have standup comedy and filmmaking in our **skill stack**. How could we further multiply this?

Duplicating Skills vs. Multiplying Them

Keep in mind that the advice my friend received was "hold a sign." Holding a sign does not require **skill**, and we already have people doing that.

This isn't to say that protests or holding a sign are not useful. However, we could multiply the effect of that act by adding **skills** to it, rather than simply duplicating existing **skills**.

I multiplied the effect of people holding signs by adding my **skill** of filmmaking to their efforts with my film *American Circumcision*. Someone holding a sign is good, but that person reaches far more people when a filmmaking **skill stack** is added to their efforts.

Most of the people whose protests you've heard about you encountered through social media and video footage. This means that someone in their organization added the **skill** of social media or photography to the existing protest **skill stack**.

Let's go back to our hypothetical standup routine. What other skills could we add?

We could add social media to distribute the footage of his routine. We could add promotion and advertising to get more people to see his routine and video. If we were really ambitious, we could add **distribution**, and make his routine part of a comedy special on streaming or TV.

All of these increase reach and the ability to "share the message."

However, if his routine "shares the message," some people might get it – but none will be **recruited** unless he offers a way for people to give him their contact information later.

How could we increase **recruitment**?

Adding Recruitment To The Stack

The most obvious and easy way would be to have a third person in the audience who collects contact information from people who like what my friend has to say.

However, this is not very well-integrated into the act. No one wants some stranger at a comedy show badgering them for their email.

The comedian could reference this person as an organizer during his act:

"My friend is always talking to me about this issue... In fact, he is in the audience tonight! Let's get a round of applause for him. You can talk to him after if you want to get involved..."

This would still require people to approach someone as something separate from the comedy event. It also might feel forced, and make the comedy act feel like an ad rather than a show.

What if instead of an organizer in the room, you sold tickets to the event and collected people's contact information as a part of the ticket checkout?

What if your organizer – instead of being present at the end – followed up with people who attended by email or phone?

Most would ignore it, but some might reply. A few might join.

This process of recruitment is not just "let me add you to my email list." The organizer would have to get to know the **skill stack** of the people he recruited so he could best use their **skills**.

Online, this process is easier.

- You could include a link with your video for people to sign up and join an organization.
- You could only share clips from the video and offer the full comedy performance for free – if they sign up for your email list.
- You could sell the performance (and take in **money**) and collect contact information at checkout.

Targeting Passive Allies

Right now, this comedy act is targeting general standup audiences.

These audiences likely have a mix of perspectives.

How could we use this act to target **passive allies** and **neutral** people who are most likely to be recruited?

Supposed my friend came to this issue through an organizer. He tells the organizer he has a standup comedy routine he has developed around this issue.

Are there events with people who are likely to be **recruited** that the organizer could place this routine at?

Of course there are. Birth-related events, men's conferences, natural health events, comedy events targeting certain audiences, etc. all might be more likely to have audiences pre-disposed to hear an Intactivist message.

If we turn this routine into **media**, the same principles apply. All of those live events **targeting** certain audiences have publications and social media pages that could share this routine.

This isn't to say you shouldn't do **neutral platforms** for the general public. Do *both*. However, if the **intention** is easy **recruiting**, some **platforms** will be better than others.

Of course, this would require the organizer to have a **skill** connecting people. He would have to know people at those events, be able to book his guy, and get the contact list of attendees to follow up.

Greater Skill Stack Creates Greater Impact

Do you see how each **skill** we added to the stack increased the impact of the effort?

People have suggested my film *American Circumcision* has had a dramatic impact for this issue. Whatever impact my film has had, it is the result of a **skill stack**.

Filmmaking itself is a **skill stack**. To make a documentary, you have to be good at cinematography, editing, interviewing subjects, etc. You also have to understand some of the business side of film.

However, my film is not just the result of my **skill stack** but other's skills as well. I can't write music, so I had to hire a composer. Some jobs I was capable of doing, but other people had greater **skill**, so I worked with them.

Plus, everyone who appears in the film brings their own perspective and expertise. I call it "my film," but the film is almost entirely other people sharing their perspectives.

The **distribution** of my film is the result of a distributor. They **organized** the **distribution** of films that had sold to Netflix before. Working with them, I knew my film would be on all the major **platforms**, who each brought their own **distribution**.

The film *American Circumcision* is the result of lots of people contributing their **resources** (**people**, **money**, **skills**) in an **organized** structure to create **media** that received high **distribution** to a **targeted** audience. It's everything we've been talking about.

The only way I could increase the impact of this film is a pop-up at the end, asking people for their contact information so they could be **recruited** into an **organization**. (Movie **platforms** aren't built to do this, but thankfully many viewers have **recruited** themselves after seeing the film.)

If you want as high an impact, follow the same structure.

High-impact events are the result of highly organized skill stacks.

Any high-impact effort will require highly **skilled** people working together in **organization**.

Even if you have the **skills** to work as a **lone operator**, **organization** will increase the impact of your **skills**.

I could have distributed my film myself. However, the **skill stack** of a distributor greatly increased the impact of my film.

And who knows? Maybe it could have had an even bigger impact if I'd had greater **resources** (**people**, **skills**, **money**) for publicity, advertising, etc. and been able to add even more **skills** to that **skill stack**.

How To Increase Your Skill Stack

Given that **skills** are the key to high-impact efforts, how do we increase our **skill stack**?

There are four ways to increase your **skill stack**:

- **Training**
- **Collaboration**
- **Recruitment**
- **Money**

First, **training**.

Training

Training is when you learn a new skill.

Virtually any **skill** you want to acquire can be learned. There are schools for it, free training online, etc. Even something like a law degree, medical training, or academic credentials can be acquired if you are determined enough.

This book is a form of **training**. I am teaching you a way of thinking about activism and **organizing** that will hopefully increase your **skill**.

People admire the Civil Rights movement, but did you know many members of that movement, including Rosa Parks, attended the Highlander Folk School, where they received activist training?

Many of the historical events people think of as spontaneous change due to moral rightness were the result of careful activist planning and **training**.

When other activists mimic the style of Civil Rights protests, they often miss the underlying **organizing** and **training** that went into them. They do not have as big an impact because they don't have the **skill stack**.

Mimicking the style of other successful movements without taking their **training** and developing their **skill stack** is like dressing up in an army costume without going to boot camp. It won't win the war.

Most activist **organizations** eventually develop some form of **training**. There are entire schools of community organizing, books on activism, and more. Activism is a **skill** you can learn, and I would encourage you to study from these sources.[2]

---

[2] If you want further activist training, visit my website here:
https://www.brendonmarotta.com/furthertraining

The advantage of training is that your **people** get better. **Training** turns **people** into **skills**.

If you have dedicated **people** in your movement who show up at every event and are lifelong members in the cause, it might be worth investing in their **training**.

Like **media**, there is an upfront cost to **training**. However, **training** pays off over time, because instead of spending years practicing a "share the message" strategy one person at a time, a trained person will become an **organizer**, **recruiter**, creator of **media**, etc.

Training Stacks Skills

Every **skill** you add increases your **skill stack** and the exponential effect of all the skills you have.

If you have a **skill** as an academic researcher, that is useful. If you add public speaking to that **skill stack**, your effectiveness increases.

An academic researcher who can appear on camera or at live events and address the public is exponentially more useful than an academic who is not well-spoken, or a public speaker with no academic credentials.

The best **skills** to **train** are ones that leverage your existing **skills**. For example, if I added a medical degree to my **skill stack**, it would not leverage my existing **skills** much compared to the **resources** required to get a medical degree. However, I already have writing in my **skill stack**, so learning about book publishing leverages that **skill** significantly.

Different **skills** require different amounts of time to acquire. However, most **skills** which do not require a four year degree usually only take six months to become proficient in.

That means if you are going to be involved in this issue for more than five years, you could acquire ten new **skills** during that time. How much more effective would you be with ten more major **skills**?

That said, there is a limit to the number of **skills** each person can acquire. Even if you acquire every **skill**, there is only so much time and energy that you have to do what you can do. Eventually, you will have to **collaborate**.

Collaborate

Collaboration is when people share **skills** and work together on a common project.

The amount of time it would take me to get a medical degree is not cost effective. However, I could **collaborate** with someone who is a doctor. He would benefit from my **skills** in creating **media**, and I would benefit from his **skills** as a medical professional.

The advantage of collaboration is that **there is no limit to the amount of skills you can add**. Each person individually can only learn so many skills. There is also only so much time during the day to use those skills. However, the more **people** you add, the more **skills** you can use.

How do you find people to collaborate with?

First, you could find them through existing **organization**. This is why **organization** is so important. Without **organization**, you cannot collaborate or **stack skills**. But how do you bring people into an **organization** to **collaborate** with?

You can **recruit** them or you can pay them (**money**).

Recruit

If you need someone with certain **skills**, you can **recruit** someone who has them.

To recruit someone, you have to **target** them with your **message**.

This could take a very informal method, like asking your friend with graphic design skills who agrees with you (**passive ally**) if he wants to help you with a project, which would make him an **active ally collaborating** with his **skills**.

However, it could also take a more formal process. If you know your **organization** is going to need a bunch of graphic designers, why not attend a graphic design conference or go on a graphic design forum and **recruit** them?

Activists intuitively understand the need for certain **skilled** professionals like doctors in their ranks. However, other **skills** like journalism, event organizing, law, non-profit fundraising, and more might be just as useful for an **organization** and easier to **recruit**.

The ability to **target** certain audiences is also a **skill**. If you want to reach a particular audience, **recruiting** someone already within that community might be useful.

As an English-speaking American, there are certain audiences I can more easily **target** than others. If I wanted to reach an Arabic-speaking Middle Eastern audience, I'd have to add fluency in a foreign language and a knowledge of local culture to my skill stack.

The much easier route would be to **recruit** someone already in the Middle East and add my media production **skills** to their **skill stack** or support them through **collaboration** with an existing **organization**.

Activists using a "share the message" model are only likely to **recruit** people in their immediate reach. This creates gaps in the audiences the movement can reach.

Non-religious English-speaking Americans are not likely to encounter Middle Eastern Arabic-speaking Muslims unless they go out of their way to specifically **recruit** those people.

However, if some foreign audiences were recruited and given the support of **organizations'** existing **skill stacks**, they could recruit more much faster.

Money For Skills

The other way to get **skilled collaborators** is to pay them (**money**).

Most professionals will work on projects they are not personally passionate about if the pay is good.

The advantage of this method is that it does not require the work of **recruiting**.

However, there are multiple disadvantages.

First, it burns **resources (money)**.

Second, the **skills** acquired are only *temporary*.

Paying someone creates a **transactional relationship**.

Transactional relationships are relationships that only continue as long as the transaction does. When the money runs out, that person will stop contributing their **skills**.

If you **recruited** someone with the same **skills**, they would contribute those **skills** for as long as they cared about the cause and there was **organization** to help them **collaborate**.

Plus, people do better work when they care about the job. Activists tend to be passionate about what they are doing. Professionals might be, but they also might just be collecting a paycheck.

This isn't to say you should never spend **money**. Some **skills** require **money**. For example, you cannot make a film without expensive equipment. You cannot buy advertising without paying the **platform** you are advertising on. However, money spent to invest in an asset will pay off more than money spent in a temporary trade.

Money For Training

Another option is to trade **money** for **training**.

If you need activists across your organization to create **media**, hiring a **media** professional to spend a day training them might be more cost effective than hiring that professional every time you need a piece of **media**.

Activists might also need less **training** than a professional has. It takes time to get a law degree, but a lawyer might be able to **train** activists with enough knowledge about the law in a single workshop to keep them out of trouble and give them the **skill** needed to run their **organization**.

Trading **money** for **training** turns the **money** into a lasting **skill** your **people** can use. It requires **organization**, because you will then need those people to use their **skills** in **collaboration**. Paying for others' **training** is not cost effective without **organization**.

If you've **recruited** someone with **skills**, they could also train others. This would accomplish the same, without the same cost as hiring a professional.

You Will Have To Collaborate

There is no other way to put it:

You will have to collaborate to end circumcision.

Even if you have the highest **skill stack** as a **lone operator**, you cannot pass a law against circumcision with only your vote. You cannot file a lawsuit and act as your own lawyer entirely alone if you want to win a big case. You won't change culture single handedly. Every path to victory requires **collaboration**.

Again, you will not win without collaboration.

To **collaborate**, you need two skills: the **skill** you are using and the **skill** of **relationships**.

Relationships are the connections between people.

If you struggle with collaboration, you need to work on relationships.

Relationships are a **skill** that can be learned.

There is a lot of **training** you can do to get better at relationships. It's one of the most difficult areas of people's lives, and the most important. Entire books, courses, and schools of thought are devoted to the challenge of how to have good relationships.[3]

Relationship Is The Most Important Skill

Training gives you access to new **skills**.

---

[3] If you'd like further resources on improving your relationships, visit my website: https://www.brendonmarotta.com/furthertraining

Relationships give you access to *others'* **skills**.

Relationships are the most important **skill** you can learn, because they give you access to every other **skill** someone in your **organization** or movement has learned.

If you don't have good **relationships**, you can't **collaborate**.

If you don't **collaborate**, you can't win.

This means **good relationships within the movement are the key to victory**.

I realize this may be hard to hear for some. Most movements have all the same relationship problems that any dysfunctional family has. Relationships are such a struggle for some people that ending circumcision might seem like an easier challenge.

However, as we've stated, relationships are a skill that can be trained. They may even be the most important skill you will ever learn in your life.

The way you improve your relationships with others is to change *your relationship to yourself*.

NEED

Why Do Activists Act Against Their Goal?

Why do activists do things that do not serve their **intention** of ending circumcision?

If **collaboration** is the key to ending circumcision, then infighting does not bring us closer to that goal. Yet anyone who has spent time around activist movements knows that there is no shortage of drama. Clashes between **organizations** and **people** are common.

Why do activists often act against their stated intention?

The answer is **hidden games**.

Hidden Games

The goal of Intactivism is to end circumcision.

This book outlines a clear path to that goal.

But what if that isn't really every activist's highest goal?

Most activists have a range of goals in their life. Yes, they want to end circumcision. However, they are also people. People want to do things like get married, have kids, advance their career, live a good life, etc.

People also have **deeper needs**. They want purpose in their life. They want to be seen and heard. They want their needs to matter to others. They want significance. They want to be loved.

Most people do not pursue their **deeper needs** directly. We rarely ask someone directly, "will you love me?" We pursue these needs indirectly. If we want love, we might spend more time with someone, share something vulnerable with them, or display attractive qualities like beauty or strength. We might ask someone out on a date.

Because these **deeper needs** are not approached directly, often we do not know what deeper need someone is pursuing. Someone might ask you out because they are seeking love. They might also be seeking validation, sex, or power over another person.

Needs pursued indirectly create **hidden games**.

Hidden games are games people play to pursue their unspoken **deeper needs**.

If one person is playing the game of seeking love, and another is playing the game of seeking validation, there might be relationship conflict. Given that each activist has a range of goals in their life, do you think activists' **deeper needs** sometimes conflict with the goals of Intactivism?

Needs Are Okay

I want to be clear about something:

All your needs are okay.

We all have **deeper needs**. Achieving the goals of the Intactivist movement does not require you to eliminate or minimize your needs. It requires you to become aware of your needs and **align** them.

Alignment is when multiple needs or people can be fulfilled by pursuing the same goal.

To make this easier, I'll share one of my **deeper needs**:

I need to be seen, heard, and understood.

Growing up, most people did not understand me. When people did not understand me, they treated me in ways that felt unsafe and created trauma. When I am not seen or heard, I feel unsafe and expect something traumatic to happen. Being seen, heard, and understood makes me feel safer and more connected to others.

Not surprisingly, this need drove me to a career in the media, where I could meet my need to be understood by sharing my reality on a larger scale. My film *American Circumcision* came in part from this need to be understood. By helping people understand the issue of circumcision, I've had part of my own trauma seen and understood.

My need to be seen and understood and the goal of Intactivism were both **aligned** to making *American Circumcision*. Making *American Circumcision* made it easier for people to see and understand me. It also created a piece of **media** that **distributed** the **message** of Intactivism across many **platforms**.

Likewise, writing this book meets both those needs. It allows me to be seen and understood by sharing my thinking, while also helping to **train** activists in **skills** that will help them better **organize** and **recruit**. Again, both my needs and the needs of the movement are **aligned**.

The problem is not our needs.

The problem is when there are needs in conflict.

Needs In Conflict

Say an activist has a **deeper need** for attention.

A second activist does something good that puts them in the spotlight and furthers the goals of the movement. The first activist, who wants attention, isn't getting attention and feels the other activist is stealing his spotlight. To meet his need for attention, he might publicly attack the activist who is in the spotlight.

Although attacking someone who is doing good hurts the goals of the movement, it fulfills the activist's **deeper need** for attention.

Now there is drama and attention on the activist who created that drama.

If the activist's **deeper need** for attention is more important to him than the needs of the movement, he might play the **hidden game** of "create drama for attention" in order to meet his **deeper need**.

However, the activist's **deeper need** for attention and the goals of the movement are in conflict. Attacking other activists might give him attention, but it hurts relationships in the movement.

These needs do not have to be in conflict.

How could we align the need for attention and the goals of the movement?

- The activist who needs attention could **collaborate** with someone in the spotlight and get attention through them.
- The activist could **recruit** people in the spotlight to his **organization**, bringing their attention with them.
- The activist who wants attention could join an **organization** already in the spotlight.
- The activist who wants attention could start a project which is so good that people give him more attention.

There are lots of potential solutions.

Needing attention is okay. The issue is the internal conflict created by pursuing that **deeper need** through a **hidden game** that is not **aligned** with the goals of the movement.

Unconscious Needs

Given that it is possible to meet deeper needs while furthering the goals of the movement, why are there ever internal conflicts?

First, people are not always aware of their **deeper needs**.

In childhood, when people shame our needs or make them not okay, we have to hide those needs and parts of ourselves. If a need is shamed enough, we might even hide it from ourselves and make it **unconscious**.

Unconscious needs are needs people have that they are not aware of.

Unconscious games are games people play that they are not aware they are playing.

Think about it. Do most people seem highly conscious to you?

Even becoming aware of the issue of circumcision requires a raise in consciousness. At one point, you were not consciously aware of this issue. When you learned more about it, you became more conscious.

Good parents help children become aware of their needs, thoughts, and feelings. However, most parents are not very aware themselves and parent children in ways that reduce their awareness rather than increase it.

If someone isn't aware of their own **deeper needs**, they might not even know why they are doing what they are doing, and they may create conflict from their lack of awareness.

Second, they may feel that it is not okay to pursue their **deeper need**.

When people are shamed for their needs, those needs do not go away. They just become hidden and pursued through **hidden games**. If someone feels their needs are not okay, they will pursue them through indirect and hidden means.

For example, many people want power. Yet it is socially unacceptable to openly seek power. Someone who wants power but feels their need is not okay might still pursue it, while framing their actions as being "for the good of others" – when they are actually just trying to gain power.

In reality, a **deeper need** for power is okay and could be aligned with the goals of the movement. A powerful person could bring far greater **resources** to any **organization** they joined. The movement could use more powerful people, and pursuing power is very much aligned with Intactivist goals.

Third, they may believe the only way to meet their needs is a **zero-sum game**.

Zero-Sum Games

Zero-sum games are games where one person wins and the other loses. Chess, boxing, and political elections are zero-sum games that people consciously choose.

Most criminal behavior is an extreme version of a **zero-sum game**. If someone mugs you and steals your wallet, they might "win" the cash in your wallet – but you lose your wallet, have your boundaries violated, and feel less safe.

Win-win games are games where both people win together. Healthy relationships are usually win-win games, where you and the other person win by becoming happier together.

Collaboration is a win-win game. If we **collaborate** on a project, I win, because you contribute skills I don't have, and you win, because I contribute skills you don't have. We both win, because we create something new that neither of us could have created alone.

If you are trying to **align**, look for **win-win** solutions.

Let's go back to our example of someone who has a **deeper need** for power.

If someone has a **deeper need** for power and believes the only way to get power is to diminish others' power (**zero-sum game**), then he will try to reduce the power of other activists to increase his own.

If someone has a **deeper need** for power and believes he can gain power by increasing others' power (**win-win game**), he will bring greater power to everyone he collaborates with, including himself.

Zero-sum games are typically learned in childhood. When parents or the people around us put their needs in conflict with ours, we learn we cannot meet their needs and ours at the same time. This forces people to play zero-sum games to meet their needs.

The Need Is Never Bad

When people play **zero-sum games**, they often hurt others.

However, the need is never bad. What causes problems is usually the **hidden game** or strategy someone is using to meet that need, their lack of awareness or honesty about their **deeper needs**, or the fact that their **deeper need** is not **aligned** with other goals.

Again, I want to reiterate:

All your needs are okay.

If someone is angry, and lashing out at others, because they have a **deeper need** to have their pain acknowledged, the problem is not that they need their pain acknowledged. The problem is that they are causing others pain as a strategy to meet their needs.

This is important because many in the Intactivist movement have experienced pain that was never acknowledged. The Intactivist movement exists because, as a child, many people were held down as someone cut off the most sensitive part of their body.

What unmet needs do you think that experience created? What needs did it make not okay to have? What might it have forced into the unconscious?

When activists want their pain acknowledged, they often seek to target **opposition** groups responsible for causing their pain and make those groups acknowledge it. These are the *least* likely people to acknowledge activists' pain, because that acknowledgement would require the furthest change for them.

Asking your opposition to meet your **deeper needs** is a bad strategy that will not win your **hidden games** or end circumcision. At best, your needs will not be met. At worst, **opposition** groups will use your actions to frame you negatively to **neutral** audiences.

Finding The Deeper Need

When people pursue **unconscious** or **hidden deeper needs**, they are often not direct about the reasons.

Most people yelling at opposition groups would say they are doing so to "end circumcision." However, we've already established that yelling at **opposition** groups is a waste of **resources** that will not end circumcision.

A more conscious answer might be, "I want the perpetrators to acknowledge my pain." There may be even **deeper needs**, like "I want to feel safe but do not feel safe knowing that people can hurt children and get away with it," or "I want them to feel pain because I'm in pain."

Some may not sound good: "I want to feel worthy. As a child, I was made to feel unworthy. People played a zero-sum game with me in which they made themselves look better by putting me down. Now, I like putting others down too by pointing out their wrongdoing, so I can feel worthy by looking morally superior to them."

That isn't a flattering statement. Yet the underlying need – "I want to feel worthy" – is okay. Once that is identified, the need can be pursued directly. How many ways could you think of to make that person feel worthy that are more **aligned** with our goals?

You have to find your own **deeper needs** and bring them into awareness. When you find a need, you can pursue it directly. Rather than playing a **hidden** or **unconscious game**, you can play a conscious one that will actually lead to meeting your needs and ending circumcision.

This requires a lot of awareness and honesty. You do not have to share what you find in this process with others if you don't want to. These needs may seem dangerous, but the only danger is when the need is **unconscious**. Once conscious, you can find ways to meet that need that create **win-win games** and are **aligned** to other goals like ending circumcision.

Meet Your Needs

Once you've found your **deeper needs**, you can resolve them consciously.

There are three ways to handle your **deeper needs**:

1) **Meet the need**. Once you've identified a need, you can pursue it directly.

    Not all your needs will be met through Intactivism. It's okay to pursue other things outside the cause that will meet your needs. If you have a way to meet your needs in your personal life, they will not conflict with activist goals or come out in unconscious ways.

2) **Heal the need**. Some deeper needs might require healing.

    Healing is anything that provides an opposite experience that resolves the need. If you were powerless, becoming empowered could be healing. If you were shamed, being accepted could be healing. If you were disconnected from others, deep connection could be healing.

If you resolve your needs through healing, they will not be unmet anymore. Your needs will not conflict with activist work when they are completely resolved. One of the reasons I advocate healing work for activists so strongly is that it completely ends entire **hidden games** by meeting the underlying need.

I have never met a person who would not benefit from healing work. Unless you were perfectly parented in an ideal community, there will be some early life needs that were not met. Those needs might still be there at an unconscious level. Some may be so powerful that *healing is the only way to resolve them*.

There are as many books, methods, and people teaching healing as there are relationships. If this is a part of your path, I encourage you to seek them. Healing is a **skill**. It can be learned. The more you do, the better you will get.[4]

3) **Align the need**. If you cannot resolve the need another way, find a way to meet it that serves the cause.

The advantage of **alignment** is that it allows you to meet your needs while doing the work. The disadvantage of **alignment** is that is must be maintained with each project.

If you know you need to feel safe, and your **hidden game** to stay safe is remaining out of the public eye, then a highly public project might make you feel unsafe and put you out of **alignment**. You will need to either find a way to feel safe in public or find a different project that is more **aligned**.

---

[4] For more on healing, check out my website:
https://www.brendonmarotta.com/furthertraining

The advantage of healing work is that it resolves the need entirely, so you do not have to worry about it again. **Alignment** must be practiced continually, with each project. It requires you to know yourself, and know what you can and can't say yes to.

No matter what you do, you will have to practice some **alignment**. If you are not aligning needs, you will have to align your **skills**. For example, I'm not aligned to projects that require a law degree. However, I'm also not aligned to projects that conflict with my **deeper needs**.

Lack of **alignment** does not mean you cannot work to end circumcision. It just means you might not be able to do every project. That's okay. Where we are not **aligned**, we find someone to **collaborate** with who is.

In my own life, I have done all three.

I have found ways to meet my needs in my personal life. I've done intense healing work on my unmet needs. I've also aligned my needs to the work I do.

These three ways of resolving needs are not contradictory but complementary. You can do more than one, and each will benefit from the other.

Recruitment Is Alignment

If someone believes that circumcision is wrong but has not taken action (**passive ally**) it is likely because they are not **aligned** to action.

Right now, when activists focus on trying to convince people to take action, they focus on "sharing the message." However, passive allies already agree with the message. They may have other objections.

"I'm not sure I can make a difference." "I don't have time." "I don't like protesting." "I don't want to talk to people." "I don't have any money to contribute." "I don't want to look stupid in public." "I'm afraid people will think I'm weird."

These are all valid feelings that if seen and understood could be **aligned** with activism.

No amount of repeating "but circumcision is really bad" will address these objections.

If you want to recruit someone, you have to listen to their **deeper needs** and find a way to **align** them with the work of your **organization**.

Once you can align your own deeper needs, then aligning the needs of others becomes easier.

It might seem like a waste of time to focus this much on internal needs. Yet as we've seen, if these needs are unmet, they come out in **hidden games** which make it harder to end circumcision and which destroy an **organization**'s ability to **collaborate**.

If we cannot **collaborate**, we cannot win. This means **aligning your needs and developing good relationships is the most important thing you can do to be an effective activist**.

Plus, these skills are going to be critical in handling both **allies** *and* **opposition**.

Need

ALLIES

Aligning Allies

Ending circumcision requires **organization**. **Organization** requires **collaboration**. **Collaboration** requires good relationships. Good relationships require **alignment**.

That means if we **align**, we win.

If we do not **align**, we lose.

The strength of our movement is the strength of our relationships.

How can we grow stronger and create greater **alignment**?

Allied Conflict

We've already established that some **allies** have conflicting needs that they pursue through **hidden games**. What should you do if an **ally** is playing a **hidden game** or even a **zero-sum game** with you?

One solution is to **align** your needs. If you can find a way to meet your needs and theirs, the game is over. **Alignment** is the best possible solution, and more likely when both parties are active allies.

In order to make **alignment** possible, you have to make it safe for the other party to have their needs. If the other person feels their need is not okay, then when you try to **align** that need, they will deny it is even there.

You could find a way to meet or heal their need. Healing requires the participation and consent of the person who needs healing. You can't "heal-rape" someone against their will. Again, if the person does not feel it is okay to even have their needs, this will not happen.

This is why I repeat throughout this book:

All your needs are okay.

When people feel their needs are okay, it becomes easier to talk about them, share them, and **align** them to the goals of the movement. This isn't just a spiritual truth but a practical strategy to ensure the movement has maximum **collaboration**, which is needed to end circumcision.

Most allied conflicts can be resolved through the above method.

However, there will be some people who refuse to find win-win solutions.

When people do so, it is usually due to **unconscious** needs that come from trauma. Those needs cause people to see situations through the lens of the situation that caused them pain. It is unlikely they will work together to resolve conflicts.

If alignment cannot be found, then there is **incompatibility**.

Incompatibility

Incompatibility is when something cannot be **aligned**.

Incompatibility does not have to be relationship ending. For example, if someone needs a professional lawyer for their project, I am **incompatible** with that role. That doesn't mean we can't **collaborate** later on a different project. It just means they need to find someone else for that job.

Likewise, just because two activists are **incompatible** does not mean either of them are bad activists. It just means they may not be able to collaborate together. **Incompatibility** can come from needs, personality conflicts, not having the right **skills**, or any number of things. If two people are genuinely **incompatible**, they should not collaborate.

Genuine **incompatibility** is rare. The more aware you are of your own needs and the better you become at **alignment**, the easier it will be to **collaborate**.

Usually, if two people are experiencing **incompatibility**, it is just because they are in the wrong roles. For example, if two people both have a need to be in charge, you could create compatibility by having them each be in charge of something, rather than putting one over the other in hierarchy.

Sometimes, though, these measures will not work. What do you do in the most extreme cases of **incompatibility**?

Toxic Personalities

The most extreme cases of **incompatibility** usually involve a **toxic personality**.

A **toxic personality** is someone whose **unconscious needs** are creating **hidden zero-sum games** that work against the goal of ending circumcision.

Imagine there is a **toxic personality** within the movement who is constantly tearing others down, behaving in abusive ways, and reducing your ability to **collaborate**.

People have spoken to them about their behavior, but they refuse to look at whatever **unconscious needs** might be causing their actions or change the **hidden zero-sum games** they use to pursue them. What should you do?

End the relationship.

I realize this may be difficult. For much of its history, the Intactivist movement has struggled to find people willing to do the work of activism. We've had to take who we can get. The idea of turning anyone away from your **organization** might seem scary.

However, if the goal is to end circumcision, people who work against that goal will not get you there, no matter how much they agree or "share the message."

Toxic personalities reduce your ability to **recruit**. Emotionally healthy **skilled** people do not want to be around **toxic personalities**. They will not join **organizations** who have them, and might leave **organizations** because of them. **Toxic personalities** will drain your **resources**.

Plus, **toxic personalities** tend to **recruit** other **toxic personalities**. For example, a narcissist will recruit co-dependents. Someone with weak boundaries will recruit people who violate those boundaries. A predator will recruit prey.

If you let a **toxic personality** represent your **organization** long enough, pretty soon your **organization** will be full of **toxic personalities**.

Please note: This does not mean you have to be perfect.

I have experienced every issue I talk about in this book. You don't have to fix every issue you have with co-dependency, boundaries, or whatever else you struggle with before becoming an activist. You simply have to make sure those issues do not drive your **organization** further from the goal of ending circumcision.

This also does not mean you have to agree with other activists on every issue. Intactivists come from every background and belief system. The only requirement to working to end circumcision is that you are **aligned** to the goal of ending circumcision. The rest is irrelevant as long as it does not conflict with that goal.

Toxic personalities are a worst case scenario. Most relationships can be aligned. While it might be tempting to abandon relationship every time conflict arises, seek **alignment** first, because we will not win without **collaborative** relationships.

What makes someone a **toxic personality** is that they take us further from the goal of ending circumcision. They might say they agree and "share the message," but their behavior is the same as **opposition**.

In fact, what are **opposition** groups but **toxic personalities** with **incompatible** needs?

Allow People To Change

Before we talk about engaging **opposition** groups, it is important to know two things.

First, it is possible for people to change.

A **toxic personality** might meet their needs, find healing, or find alignment. You might also change, creating compatibility and alignment where there previously was none.

Plus, people change their position on the **spectrum of allies**. Although it takes greater change, it is possible for **opposition** to become **ally**. Many of the greatest **allies** in the movement are doctors who used to circumcise and stopped, regret parents who circumcised their kids and realized they were wrong, and people who come from circumcising cultures that questioned those cultures.

We must always leave the door open for **opposition** to become an **ally**, or **toxic personalities** to change and become **collaborative**.

This doesn't mean you have to trust every **toxic person** who says "I've changed" and let them re-enter your life or **organization**. However, it does mean giving them the opportunity to demonstrate their change through meaningful action that brings **resources** to the movement.

If someone says "I've changed" but acts the same, they have not really changed. If someone says "I've changed" and turns their change into a **message** that **recruits** people, starts **collaborating** in healthy **relationships**, and takes steps in their personal life to meet and heal their needs, then maybe they have.

Find Likely Allies

Second, you do not *have* to have relationship with most opposition groups.

The biggest gains come from **recruiting**, **organizing**, and **collaborating** with **passive allies**. You can start a successful **organization** without ever directly engaging **opposition**.

If you aren't talking to **opposition**, who are you talking to?

Likely allies.

Likely allies are people, groups, or **organizations** who are currently **neutral** but are likely to become an **ally**. Likely allies often have other beliefs that **pre-suade** them to become an ally.

Pre-suasion is any belief or concept that makes someone predisposed to accept a new idea they are not yet convinced of.

For example, someone who supports natural birth is a **likely ally** for Intactivism. Natural birth advocates believe that many birth interventions are unnecessary and harmful.

If you believe "many birth interventions are harmful," that acts as **pre-suasion** for Intactivism, because it is not a huge leap to go from that belief to believing circumcision is one of those harmful birth interventions.

Intactivists have numerous **likely allies**.

I have seen people come to Intactivism through natural birth, veganism, atheism, new age spirituality, social justice politics, conservative politics, sex positivity, gender issues, and the list goes on and on.

Some **likely allies** even come from groups who disagree on other issues, like feminists and men's rights activists.

These activists do not have to be **aligned** on other issues. However, if you are recruiting someone, you must **pace** their current beliefs.

Stay On Message

When activists come from other issues, they sometimes bring those unrelated issues with them.

If you bring up other issues, and your intended target shares your beliefs, that is a **pace**. For example, a Christian Intactivist might reference his faith when talking to another Christian, because it makes it easier to **lead** that person to a new idea about circumcision.

However, bringing up other issues alienates potential allies who do not share your beliefs. If a Christian Intactivist were to demand an atheist convert to Christianity before becoming an Intactivist, he would alienate that potential **ally**.

When Intactivists mix issues or place ideological requirements on the movement beyond opposing circumcision, they limit their ability to **recruit** from – and even cut themselves off from – potential **resources**.

Stay on message.

The way to know your **message** is to remember your **intention**. Is your goal to **recruit** this person for Intactivism? Will bringing up unrelated issues **pace** them or alienate them? If unrelated issues are not a **pace**, then **stay on message**.

If your other issue is so important that you have to talk about it, go through the same process we've outlined for Intactivism:

Find **likely allies**. Listen to them. **Pace** their beliefs. Don't yell at **opposition** or people who will not change. That includes people who are **allies** on Intactivism but **opposition** on your unrelated issues.

If your other issue is so important that you must do activism for it, do it right.

Align Your Recruits

Where you **recruit** is important because each group of **likely allies** brings certain **skills** – but also certain needs.

For example, it might be easy to **recruit** fringe conspiracy theorists because the belief that all mainstream institutions are lying is good **pre-suasion** for the idea that some of those institutions should also not be trusted on circumcision.

However, if you were to focus on recruiting fringe conspiracy theorists, then you'd have a movement full of fringe conspiracy theorists. If those **allies** do not **stay on message**, they will likely alienate many potential **recruits**.

Fringe conspiracy theorists are not known for having a lot of **skills** or **money**. While this might be an easy **target** for **recruiting,** how much closer does it bring us to ending circumcision? Plus, if any of those fringe conspiracy theorists are **toxic personalities**, bringing them in actually harms the movement.

This isn't to say you cannot **recruit** people with strange beliefs. There are many effective activists who hold unconventional beliefs the majority of the world does not share. They just don't talk about those unrelated issues when they are representing the movement.

If you **recruit** people from other issues, take the time to **align** them and **train** them to **stay on message**. If you don't, they could end up costing more **resources** than they bring in.

When **targeting**, you are looking for people who have high **resources** and are **likely allies**.

Although fringe conspiracy theorists might be easy **targets**, most have low **resources**. It might cost more **resources** to **train** them to **stay on message** than they bring in.

A better target might be harder to reach, but will be more **resource** effective, because the people you recruit will bring more **resources** and require less investment in **training**.

Whoever you **recruit** must be **aligned** with the goals of Intactivism and **stay on message**.

Building The Coalition

In order to end circumcision, you will have to work with people who disagree with you on other issues, because Intactivism is a **coalition**.

A **coalition** is a group of **organizations** or movements aligned towards a particular goal.

There is no one **organization** or belief system that unites all of Intactivism beyond the shared goal to end circumcision. People come from every background or belief system. You do not have to be **aligned** with every aspect of a person to **collaborate** with them, just the aspects relevant to your shared goal.

You will never reach a majority without engaging people you disagree with.

The world is a big place. There are a lot of different perspectives, and each person you talk to has their own. **Collaborating, aligning**, and having good **relationships** requires recognizing others' perspective as valid while sharing your own.

You might need to remind people:

All your needs are okay.

And then see if we can meet those needs together.

Aligned Collaboration

This chapter talks a lot about how to handle **allies** that are out of **alignment**.

What does it look like when they are **aligned**?

The best collaborations are free from **hidden games**.

If I need to get **aligned**, I **align** myself.

If you need to get **aligned**, you do the same.

If we can't do it alone, we do it together.

Then we just try stuff, see what works, and play the game.

Aligned relationships are actually very simple. It's **unaligned** relationships that are complex and draining. Once you are aligned, **collaboration** is easy.

If you spend a lot of time with collaborators doing something other than the stated game of the project, it's a sign something is **unaligned** and causing **hidden games**.

Needing **alignment** is okay.

All your needs are okay.

If you are not **aligned**, find the need and **align** it.

If we **align**, we win.

The strength of our movement is the strength of our relationships.

Engaging The Opposition

Most of the work lies in **aligning allies**.

However, you will eventually have to engage **opposition**.

There is no way to pass a law without engaging the political system.

There is no way to file a lawsuit without engaging the court system.

There is no way to change culture without engaging the culture.

Opposition groups already have a strong foothold in all of these areas.

When you meet them, what will you do?

OPPOSITION

Internal Is External

A friend of mine who had studied both martial arts and healing arts once told me that the same pressure points you strike in combat are the ones you soothe in massage.

The body is the body, and knowledge of bodywork intended to heal translated into bodywork intended to harm.

He told me:

If you can heal, you can kill.

The same is true in our work. If you understand how to **recruit** and **align** your **allies** in **organization**, then you already know how to destroy your **opposition**.

Just do the opposite.

Opposition Is Needs In Conflict

The needs opposition groups have are legitimate.

When I say "**all your needs are okay,**" that applies to *everyone*.

For example, circumcising medical groups want to be seen as good. They want to make money. They do not want to be exposed to liability. All of these needs are okay.

Circumcising religious and ethnic groups want to feel safe. They want to avoid bigotry and harassment. They want to maintain their unique identity and tribe. All of these needs are okay.

The issue of opposition groups is not their needs. It is needs in *conflict*.

See how our internal knowledge applies to the external game as well?

There are ways we could find a **win-win** with all opposition groups.

It would be possible for medical groups to end circumcision in a way that looked good for them, did not expose them to liability, and still made them money.

It would be possible for ethnic and religious groups to end circumcision in a way that felt safe for them and still maintained their unique identity.

If you are **opposition** and reading this book, I want you to know I'm open to finding **win-win solutions** together. It will require each of us to see and understand the other's needs, recognize them as valid, and work together to find **alignment** where both of our needs are met. It may sound challenging, but it is possible.

However, most **opposition** groups are not looking for a **win-win**. They are playing a **zero-sum game**, with the attitude that since they have greater **resources (people, money, skills)** they don't have to consider Intactivist needs.

What do you do when someone else is playing a **zero-sum game** with you?

What Game Does Opposition Play

When someone is playing a zero-sum game with you, you have three options:

1) **Align to a win-win**.

  If you can find a scenario where opposition feels they have won, they may not care if you win also. When doctors suggest that activists should "talk to the parents," what they are really saying is that they want activists to pursue their needs in a way that requires no change from them.

This is unlikely, since finding **win-win solutions** usually requires both participants. Even if Intactivists find a solution that meets doctors' stated needs, there may be **unconscious needs** we are not aware of that cause them to reject those solutions.

If you want to find a **win-win solution** with **opposition**, you will have to create relationships with **opposition** groups. This is nearly impossible if they do not want a relationship with you. Expecting activists to find a win-win outside of relationship or meaningful communication is unreasonable and unlikely.

2) **End the relationship**.

You do not have to have a relationship with **opposition**.

Do not visit doctors who practice or support circumcision. Have your child with a doula or natural birth professional that does not practice circumcision. Do not support or contribute to organizations that support circumcision, even passively.

When you end your relationship with **opposition organizations**, let them know why. Tell them you will consider connecting with them again when they become **allies** on this issue, leaving the door open for change.

There is no reason to give your **resources** to **opposition** when **allied** services exist. If the path to ending circumcision involves **organizing resources**, giving your **resources** to **opposition** works against this goal.

However, there may be spaces where you have to engage opposition. What do you do then?

3) **Win the game**.

This is harder.

To win the game, you have to understand the game you are playing.

The Game Of Opposition

We've already talked about how even **allies** have **hidden games**. This is especially true of **opposition** groups.

For example, doctors' groups state that their intention is to do what is best for children. In practice, there is a **hidden game** they play to acquire status and wealth. They may say their primary goal is to heal children, yet when that goal conflicts with the need for money, they often choose money.

To understand **opposition**, do not look at what they say. Look at what they do.

The best indicator of future behavior is past behavior.

How has **opposition** handled past conflicts?

Previous Opposition Conflicts

Let's look at the strategy the medical establishment has used against a different movement: the anti-vaccination movement.

(We are looking at this purely to understand the **hidden game** of medical organizations, not to evaluate the rightness or wrongness of either side. This is purely strategic analysis. I am choosing this conflict as an example only because it includes mutual **opposition** groups.)

Did the medical establishment yell at anti-vaccination groups to stop?

No. They went after **neutral** institutions.

The medical establishment got Amazon to stop selling anti-vaccination documentaries and got Facebook to delete anti-vaccination groups and ban fundraising for anti-vaccination **organizations**.

Amazon and Facebook are **neutral** institutions that were acting as **passive allies** to the anti-vaccination movement by hosting their media and providing a **platform** to **organize**. The medical establishment moved them from **neutral** to their side of the spectrum.

They also went after the anti-vaccination movements' biggest method for generating leads by **targeting** their **message** and turned those leads into **resources**. In military terms, this is what's known as cutting the supply lines.

Basically, medical organizations destroyed the anti-vaccination movements' ability to **message**, **recruit**, **organize**, and get **resources** from the largest **neutral platforms** available to them.

Disrupt The Opposition

The game of **opposition** is to capture **neutral** institutions.

First, notice how this strategy is different than what the Intactivist movement would use.

If Intactivists were playing the pro-vaccine medical establishment's side with their "share the message" strategy, they would use the medical establishment's resources to "share the message" that vaccines are good.

The medical establishment has done this too with their #VaccinesWork message, but it's not the only thing they are doing. They are using the organizer model for their side, while *actively destroying their opposition's ability to organize*.

Like we said earlier, if you know how to heal, you know how to kill. If you know how to **organize**, you also know how to **disrupt**.

Disruption is when you destroy your **opposition**'s ability to practice any step of the organizer model – **message**, **recruit**, **organize**, acquire **resources**, reach **platforms**, etc.

How does the **opposition disrupt?**

Toxic Branding

The primary strategy of **opposition** groups to **disrupt** enemy organizing is **toxic branding**.

We've already talked about **toxic personalities** within a movement.

Toxic branding is when you frame a person, organization, or entire movement as someone people should end their relationship with.

The first **toxic brand** the medical establishment tried on the anti-vaccination movement was "anti-science." They framed anti-vaccination groups as not just being wrong, but opposed to scientific reasoning entirely.

However, this did not stick, because "anti-science" is not a **toxic brand**.

Most Americans have some beliefs that could be framed as unscientific. Furthermore, people don't **end relationships** over scientific disagreement. Odds are, you have some friends whose beliefs you disagree with, but you still love them all the same.

Another reason the brand didn't stick was that it could be refuted with scientific-sounding arguments.

Anti-vaccination activists spend more time reading the scientific literature on vaccines than the general public. It is very easy for an anti-vaccination activist to sound scientific to most audiences, which meant all those activists had to do to shake the brand "anti-science" was to get their **message** out.

When the "anti-science" brand did not work, the medical establishment began branding the anti-vaccination movement as "violent."

The medical establishment said the anti-vaccination movement was using "violent rhetoric" and engaging in "threatening" behavior. They referred to anti-vaccination activism as "harassment" and claimed their "violent rhetoric" would somehow lead to real world violence.

The goal of this branding is not to stop "violence." If you actually fear violence, you go to the police, not social media. The goal of "violent" branding is to make anti-vaccination groups **toxic** and cause **neutral** institutions and **platforms** to end their relationship with them.

People do not end their relationships when someone is "unscientific." They do end their relationships when someone seems "violent."

Plus, there is a network effect. If someone sees you as an **ally** to people who are violent, might they also end their relationship with you?

Toxicity Spreads

If you become branded as toxic, that brand can spread to your allies.

Opposition groups do not brand people as **toxic** in order to **target** them. They brand people as toxic in order to target their **allies**.

When the medical establishment branded anti-vaccination groups as "violent," they didn't go to those groups and ask them to change. They went to **neutral platforms** like Amazon and Facebook and asked, "Why are you allowing violent anti-science ideas to be promoted on your platform?"

Neutral institutions do not have the time or interest to research every topic. Claims that a movement is right or wrong will have little effect on them. However, they do not want to be associated with "violent" people. If they are seen as associating with **toxic people**, then they too could become **toxic**.

Shared Allies

Medical organizations also didn't go to **neutral platforms** directly.

They went through **shared allies**.

Shared allies are people or organizations that are allies to more than one group.

The first people to talk to social media platforms about anti-vaccination content were politicians and journalists who were **allies** of the medical industry.

Social media companies needed these politicians and media outlets as their **allies**. They did not need anti-vaccination groups the same way. By flexing the influence of their **coalition**, the medical establishment de-**platformed** the anti-vaccination movement.

Do you see how different this strategy is from the "share the message" way of thinking? How many Intactivists would use a **shared ally** to get a **neutral** institution to **disrupt** an **opposition organization**?

This is three steps removed from the activist, but look at the range of change required.

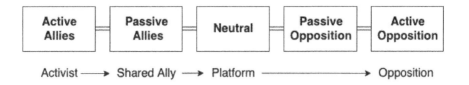

In each case, the activist is only required to influence and **target** an adjacent group, while the neutral **platform** being asked to end a relationship with someone as far as possible from them on the spectrum.

The activist is **disrupting opposition organizations** from the safest distance and strongest position.

Intactivists have done this before. For example, the National Secular Society was able to get Amazon UK to stop selling circumcision training devices.

The National Secular Society is not an explicitly Intactivist institution, but it does include some **shared allies**, making it part of the Intactivist **coalition**.

When they wrote to Amazon, they didn't say "circumcision is bad." They said that Amazon did not want to make their brand **toxic** by selling unsafe medical devices to the public.

Intactivists have not been able to achieve the same result with Amazon in the United States because they approach Amazon as **lone operators** rather than as an **organization**. They approach through **active allies** rather than **shared allies**. Many also argue from the message "circumcision is bad," rather than "this is **toxic branding**."

Some activists show an intuitive understanding of toxic branding when they use negative names for circumcising groups.

However, these names are not well-**targeted**. Usually, they are hurled at **active opposition** from **active allies**. To be effective, they need to come from **shared allies** targeting **neutral platforms**.

How To Fight A Toxic Brand

How do you respond when someone attempts to **toxically brand** you?

The first question to consider is, how effective was the branding?

Branding shares all the same challenges as **messaging**:

- How big a **platform** do they have?
- What is their **distribution**?
- Who are they **targeting**?
- Did they **recruit** anyone?

You do not have to respond to every account with under a hundred followers that calls you a bad name. In fact, you should not.

There is a principle in public relations: Respond to attacks that come from bigger **platforms**, but *not* ones that come from smaller **platforms**.

Let's say an account with 100 followers attacks you, and you have 10,000 followers. At worst, 100 people have seen one **message** branding you as **toxic**.

If you respond, not only have those 100 people seen the message, your 10,000 followers are also talking about it. You've essentially **platformed** the **opposition**.

Secondly, how well-**targeted** was the attack? An anti-Intactivist page probably doesn't reach **allies** or even **neutral** groups. **Opposition** groups are often only talking to **opposition** audiences.

I understand why Intactivists might want to respond. The labels opposition groups often use are clearly wrong, intentionally hurtful, and easily refuted.

However, responding increases the **platform** of the **message**. You would be better off using your platform to spread your **message**.

If the toxic branding was not **distributed** to your audience, it didn't happen.

Activists often worry about the **toxic branding opposition** will try to attach to them. However, there are only a few **platforms** where such a brand could be **distributed** that would make it relevant. Even in the instances where a lone accuser takes down a public figure, they usually do so with the **distribution** of **media**.

Most **toxic branding** can be avoided by branding yourself well.

Targeted Toxicity

Who is **targeted** by **toxic branding**?

Opposition usually goes after two types of **targets** with **toxic branding**:

- **Easy targets**
- **High-resource targets**

Easy targets are people easily branded as **toxic**. If someone is already acting **toxic**, it's not hard for **opposition** to point out their **toxic** behavior.

We all know what statements or behaviors the **opposition** will jump on to frame Intactivists as **toxic**. If you want to avoid **toxic branding**, don't make yourself an **easy target**.

However, even if you act in a way that is beyond reproach, that won't stop **opposition** from framing normal people as **toxic**. This is politics. If they can't find something, they'll make it up.

The second category **opposition** will go after is **high-resource targets**.

High-resource targets are people who bring a lot of **resources** into the movement. They might also be leaders in the movement or in charge of **organizations**.

Opposition will go after the leaders of a movement whether or not they are actually **toxic**, because if they can brand the leadership as **toxic**, it will significantly **disrupt** the **organization** and **resources** of the entire movement.

However, people in leadership roles tend to not make themselves **easy targets**, because they know that **opposition** will try to **disrupt** them. Likewise, the kind of people who make themselves **easy targets** usually do not have a lot of **resources**, nor do they achieve leadership roles.

So what does opposition do?

They try to tie an **easy target** to a **high-resources target**.

Fabricated Toxicity

Anyone who wants can go online, make a fake account claiming to be a part of someone else's movement, and start spewing vile hateful statements at people.

Likewise, it's not hard to show up at a protest, get someone to give you a sign, and then start engaging in **toxic** behaviors.

Easy targets are easy to create because the **barrier to entry** for most movements is low. Online, this barrier is virtually zero.

When opposition wants to brand **high-resource targets**, they will often try to tie the behavior of **easy targets** to the leadership.

For example, one journalist who did a biased story on circumcision shared a piece of anonymous hate mail she received to her sixty thousand followers to frame those against circumcision as "trolls."

When actual public figures in the Intactivist movement responded to her with kind, thoughtful responses, she completely ignored them. Those responses did not support the **toxic branding** she was trying to give people who disagreed with her, so she had no interest in **platforming** them.

If you want to know why the media doesn't interview kind, thoughtful Intactivists, it's *because* they're kind, thoughtful Intactivists. **Opposition** media is not looking for people who would brand the movement as kind or thoughtful. They are looking for **easy targets**.

This is unfair branding. Random accounts on the internet do not represent an **organization**. Plus, **opposition** groups rarely hold themselves to the same standard when pro-circumcision accounts engage in **toxic** behavior. However, this doesn't stop them from using the tactic.

Remember, the goal of **toxic branding** is to persuade **neutral** audiences or **platforms** to end their relationship with you. It doesn't matter if the branding is true or false. What matters is the relationship.

You might have heard it said that "you can win the argument, but lose the relationship." The same is true in activism. You might not have done anything wrong, but what matters are the feelings of **neutral** audiences and **platforms**.

Given that if **opposition** wants to **target** you, they can always just make something up, how do you prevent an attack?

Thankfully, the only thing that really matters is the **distribution** of **toxic branding**.

Distributed Toxicity

When it comes to **toxic** behaviors:

If you don't document it, it didn't happen.

I have seen activists engage in behavior that could be framed as **toxic** that was never documented or **distributed** by **opposition media**.

I have also seen activists do things that were not **toxic** that **opposition** framed as **toxic** and **distributed** through **media**.

The second category hurt the movement more, because **toxic branding** follows the same principles as **messaging**.

Just like the best **message distributed** to a room of twenty people can only lead to twenty **recruits**, the worst **toxicity distributed** to a room of twenty people can only lead to twenty people ending the relationship with you (unless those twenty **distribute** it further to others, through rumors or media).

The flip side is true as well. **Opposition** will frequently engage in **toxic** behaviors. When activists attempt to respond to their **toxicity**, opposition will rush to the media to write about how they are being "harassed" or "attacked" by "online trolls."

Even if the truth is that activists were kind, and **opposition** was **toxic**, only people who saw the original interaction know that. The rest of the world sees their narrative, **distributed** through **media**.

Again:

If you don't document it, it didn't happen.

Opposition engages in **toxic** behavior all the time. They insult activists, body shame intact men, and make sexually harassing comments.

However, activists are so used to this **toxic** behavior from **opposition**, it doesn't occur to them to document and **distribute** it to **neutral** audiences.

Opposition organizations are much more fragile here. Isn't the standard of conduct for medical and religious leaders higher than the standard for citizens protesting on the street?

Every tactic I write about in this section can be flipped. As activist Saul Alinsky said, "Make the enemy live up to its own book of rules." If the enemy wants to focus on **toxic branding** rather than the actual issue, document and **distribute opposition toxicity** to **neutral targets**.

What Is Toxicity?

We've been talking a lot of **toxic branding**, but what makes something **toxic**?

A brand is **toxic** when it causes others to end the relationship.

That's it. There is no objective definition.

There may be perspectives or behavior that you and I personally find distasteful. However, what makes something **toxic** is when your **target** audience finds it worth ending the relationship.

Different audiences find different things **toxic**. Some of what your audience finds **toxic** might not be **toxic** to you. For example, for some audiences find atheism **toxic**. Others find fundamentalist religious belief **toxic**. You have to know your audience.

Generally, the overriding principle of **toxicity** is that **toxic behavior makes people feel unsafe.**

Safe relationships are relationships where people's needs are okay. The safest relationships are ones where the other person makes your needs as important as their own.

People feel unsafe in relationship when their needs might be threatened, invalidated, ignored, misunderstood, or made not okay.

If people feel unsafe in a relationship, they will end it.

For example, if someone is branded as "violent," people will end their relationship with them, because it isn't safe to be around violent people.

However, emotional safety is just as important. If someone is branded as a "bigot," they might not physically harm anyone, but people will feel unsafe having a relationship with them, because they might discriminate against them or threaten their need for acceptance.

People might also feel unsafe in a relationship, because the relationship will cost them other relationships. A movement or idea could become **toxic** simply because other people make it unsafe for someone to adopt that idea and stay in other relationships.

If joining a movement could cost someone their job, their connection to their family, or other relationships in their life, it might feel **toxic** to them no matter how well the movement behaves.

The opposite is also true. People go towards safety in relationships. If a movement is popular, well-liked, and will gain people relationships, they might join even if they don't strongly believe in the cause.

There are many causes people pay lip service to simply because it makes them look good.

For example, there is zero social cost to saying you want to end world hunger. It's a safe relationship. However, movements that look at the underlying cause of poverty or hunger might be less safe, because they will cost other relationships.

One way to avoid toxic branding is to ask: **what can I do to create a safe relationship?**

Media Becomes Toxic

If someone attacks your safe relationship, you are liable to see the attacker as **toxic**, rather than their intended target.

Part of the reason people are less trustful of mainstream media is that the media has made people feel unsafe and developed a **toxic** reputation. If people feel that media might make them unsafe, then they will end their relationship with media. This is especially true if they see the media as **opposition** on issues they care about.

Plus, if movements can frame **media** as **toxic**, any attempt by media to brand those movements will fail. This is a huge win for movements at risk for **toxic branding**.

Mainstream media is **opposition** for many movements. At this point, there are more movements and **organizations** interested in branding mainstream media as **toxic** than preserving relationship with it.

Counter-branding is a legitimate strategy. The media has been effectively branded as **toxic** to many **neutral** audiences. This means that when the media attacks Intactivists, Intactivists can flip that by **pacing neutral** audiences' distrust of media and use the attack to **recruit**.

The mainstream media has not created safe relationship with the Intactivist movement. They make frequent and significant errors when reporting on circumcision. Plus, **opposition** groups with greater access to the media have used media in the past to attempt to **toxically brand** Intactivists.

While Intactivists would prefer that mainstream media accurately report on this issue and create safe relationships with them, media attacks only matter for audiences that trust or read those media sources. If the attack comes from a **toxic** source, it can be easily flipped.

Conflict Is Attention

What do you do if an attempt to **toxically brand** you is well **targeted** and well **distributed**?

If an **opposition** group attacks you directly, they've given you the spotlight. You now have access to their **distribution**. Use it. This is an opportunity to **message**, and all the same principles of **messaging** apply.

Conflict is attention; attention is influence.

If someone is creating conflict with you, they are giving you their attention and the attention of their audience. You can use that attention however you like.

Humans are naturally drawn to conflict. If while reading this book, you heard a fight happening outside, you would stop to see what was going on with the fight. This book is teaching you how to end circumcision, yet two strangers engaging in fisticuffs outside could take your attention from it.

The same is true of political conflict. Corporate branding is boring. Drama is exciting. When a dozen different activists are doing things, what are people talking about? The ones starting drama.

You can use this to your advantage. When **opposition** strikes, they give you an opportunity to get your message out.

Some **opposition** groups know this and make it difficult to respond. They will attack an activist and then interview an "expert" on their **toxic branding**, rather than the activist themself. In these cases, you may have to work harder for the attention.

However, if you're on their **platform**, then they control the framing. When the **toxic branding** comes, your goal is to reframe it.

The Disavow Game

"When did you stop beating your wife?" is a classic bad framing question. Any answer you give will imply that you used to beat your wife and stopped, or that you are still beating your wife.

What about this bad framing question:

"Do you disavow the racists and antisemites in your **organization**?"

Keep mind, if you say there aren't any, **opposition** will respond that there are, and accuse you of "defending antisemitism." They will frame non-toxic behaviors as **toxic**, tie you to an **easy target**, or fabricate the **toxic** behavior entirely.

If **opposition** asks you to disavow an activist they have branded as **toxic**, what should you do?

If you chose not to disavow: Opposition runs a headline with the **toxic** activist's picture next to yours, with the headline "Activist refuses to disavow **toxic** person." They use your response to tie your brand to the **toxic** person. Every future article written about you mentions that you refused to disavow a **toxic** activist. Your brand becomes **toxic**.

If you chose to disavow: Opposition runs a headline with the **toxic** activist's picture next to yours, with the headline "Activist disavows ties to **toxic** person." They use your response to tie your brand to the **toxic** person. Every future article written about you mentions that you once had to disavow a **toxic** activist. Your brand becomes **toxic**.

This is what is known as a **magician's choice**.

A **magician's choice** is something presented as a real choice, when both options lead to the same outcome. The technique is frequently used by stage magicians but also applies to arenas that are just as fake – like politics or **media**.

Activists may think that if they disavow, the controversy will go away. However, the goal of **opposition** isn't to make the controversy go away, but to spread **toxicity**. If they have successfully branded one activist as **toxic**, then they will attempt to spread that brand to others.

If both options are bad, what do you do?

Find a third option.

Control The Frame

Magician's choices are false dichotomies. You do not have to avow or disavow every person under the sun because your **opposition** asks you to. You could easily just say, "That activist speaks only for themself, and if you'd like to talk about their work, you should interview them."

If the request to disavow is **distributed** on a small enough **platform**, you could ignore it. You could simply say that the person they are asking about has no ties to you. You could shift their attention to something else, or counter brand the group attacking you.

There are a lot of options. What you chose will depend on your circumstances, creativity, and available **resources**. However, do not accept the choices your **opposition** presents as your only choices.

Even if you come up with the best answer to "Do you disavow **toxic** people?" you are still arguing in the frame of the question "Are you **toxic**?" What does this associate your brand with?

Intactivists want to argue within the frame of Intactivism. When Intactivists argue within the frame of Intactivism, they win. **Opposition** groups will attempt to frame the debate as being about anything but the issue Intactivists are raising, because they cannot win on that ground.

This means that when **opposition** attempts to **disrupt** and distract you, you must reframe.

Here is an example of a reframe: "Why are you trying to silence the voices of our Jewish members?" Now the frame is, "Is your **opposition** trying to silence Jewish victims of genital cutting?" Whatever they answer, we aren't talking about how you might be **toxic** anymore. We're talking about their **toxic** behavior.

Note that this still frames the discussion in the context of Jewish people. This is useful, because it **paces** their attack a bit, but you could reframe even further. "Hundreds of children die every year from circumcision, and you want to talk about offensive words. Why don't their deaths matter to you?"

Where you reframe to depends on where you want to draw your audience's attention. The first flip directs their attention to Jewish activists, the second to circumcision deaths. You could create a flip to take the discussion to any aspect of this issue you want.

Opposition accusations are intended not to solve **toxic** behavior but to associate you with it. They like when activists behave in ways they can brand as **toxic**, because it allows them to dismiss legitimate activists' concerns. They are not making honest claims but playing a **hidden game**, and you do not have to play their game by their rules.

Flip The Attack

What do you do when **opposition** lands a well-**targeted**, well-**distributed, toxic branding**?

Pace, **lead**, and flip the **message**.

To **pace**, you have to know what your audience is currently thinking. However, if **opposition** media published a big **message** about you, you can safely assume their audience is thinking about that **message**. This gives you an opportunity to **lead**.

Pace. You saw them say this. **Lead**. In reality, this is true.

It is important to address the misconceptions, because if you don't, you are just **leading**. **Pacing** is how you show people you understand their reality, fears, and current beliefs. Right now, they just heard you were **toxic**. Address that.

Be careful of too big a **lead**. "They said that because the media is run by people who hate children!" Will your audience really follow you there? All the same principles of **messaging** apply. Start where people are and take them one step along the spectrum at a time.

Branding is just **messaging**. One message can be undone by another. If the **opposition** has given you a **toxic** brand, you may have to lead people further, but it can be done.

Safe Relationship

All opposition strategies are about destroying your relationships.

If you've ever had a **toxic personality** attempt to destroy your relationships, you know it only works on people susceptible to it. Usually, when a **toxic** personality can destroy your other relationships, it is because they are able to exploit a problem in the existing relationship.

For example, if an **ally** is jealous of your success, a toxic personality might tell them it's because you do not value them. If your friend genuinely does not feel valued, and does not have safety in relationship to talk to you about that problem directly, you could lose that relationship.

However, if your friend has a strong bond with you and a safe relationship, no amount of scheming from **toxic personalities** can break that relationship. True friends stand by you.

Safe relationships are relationships where all your needs are safe.

The solution to opposition toxicity is to create safe relationships.

This includes relationships within the movement and relationships with others.

The strength of our movement is the strength of our relationships.

Unfortunately, many in the Intactivist movement have not had safe relationships.

For some, their families did not understand or protect them on the first days of their life. For others, their families rejected them when they shared their feelings about circumcision. Even those who have no trauma around circumcision likely have little experience with safe relationships, because unsafe relationships are the default relationship of the world.

This is why I say:

All your needs are okay.

Opposition Relationships

In recent years, I have heard some pro-circumcision voices complain that people do not feel comfortable speaking out in favor of circumcision because of the backlash from Intactivists.

This complaint always struck me as strange, because no amount of backlash could silence me, nor most activists I know.

There are religious believers who die as martyrs rather than renounce their faith. There are human rights activists who do their work in countries where it is illegal to do their work. There are people who live their truth even if it means being disowned by their family.

When people truly believe something, no consequence can stop them.

Most Intactivists I know have faced some consequences for their activism, even if it is just a drain on their **resources** because they put their own money and time into the cause.

The fact that mean comments on the internet can deter **opposition** shows that they do not really believe what they are saying.

After all, most **opposition** groups come from **transactional relationships**.

Transactional relationships only continue as long as the transaction does. Medical organizations would not perform circumcisions if they stopped getting paid to do them.

When doctors complain that they do far more than circumcisions, what they are really protesting is that something which brings in only a few **resources** might cost them a lot more. However, that's the point: It should cost them.

Relationships among circumcising ethnic and religious groups like Judaism or Islam might look stronger, but in some ways they are more conditional. If a person stops believing or supporting the tribe, the relationship ends.

Membership in these communities has great benefits, but the underlying message is that love is conditional, and that they can lose their relationship if they do not fulfill the will of the tribe.

Win-win is possible here. Doctors can get paid, and be against circumcision. People can be members of a tribe, and against circumcision. However, if needs are in conflict, these relationships will fall.

Remember: *If you can heal, you can kill.*

If you know how to create safe relationships, you know how to **disrupt opposition** relationships.

Is the desire to cut children's genitals really aligned with other **opposition** needs? With **neutral** institutions? With the **shared allies** of those institutions? Can these needs be thrown into conflict? Are **opposition** relationships really that safe?

Everything we've talked about in this chapter can be flipped.

Playing The Opposition's Game Against Them

What would it look like if you played the **opposition**'s game against them?

Right now, **opposition** groups have more resources than Intactivist groups. If they could spend ten dollars of their **resources** to destroy every dollar of ours, they'd probably consider it a bargain. You won't win going dollar for dollar.

In the majority cases, building a **coalition** of **allies** is the more effective use of **resources**. However, if you are going to create conflict, use it to gain **resources** and seize **neutral** institutions.

Remember: *Conflict is attention and attention is influence*. Conflict is a way to get the **message** out, yet that **message** is only useful if it is **targeted** to **recruit**, or targeted at **neutral** institutions through **shared allies**. Just yelling at the **opposition** is a waste of **resources**.

Even if you chose to take the route of conflict, you will want to spend the majority of your time creating **allies**, because those **shared allies** are how you will **disrupt** the enemy.

When Jewish **organizations** sought to oppose the SF MGM bill, a ballot initiative that would have criminalized the circumcision of minors in San Francisco, the first thing they did was create a **coalition** against it. This **coalition** included many religious and human rights **organizations** that had no ideological reason to support circumcision. Some, like the ACLU, had reasons to oppose it. However, prior to the conflict, Jewish **organizations** had recruited these groups into their **coalition** for other issues.

Pro-circumcision organizations won that conflict using the principles outlined in this book. They were better **organized**, built a larger **coalition**, gathered more **resources**, put their **message** out in **media**, branded their **opposition** as **toxic**, and then ended the ballot initiative through lawsuits and passed pro-circumcision legislation at the state level.

"Share the message" activists didn't stand a chance.

If Intactivists want to win future conflicts with **opposition**, this is the process:

When you engage in conflict, make sure your relationships are strong and safe. Build your **coalition** and **align** your **allies** first. Gather **resources**. Pick a **target** that will gain you **recruits** or seize a **neutral** institution from the **opposition**. Use **shared allies** to get closer to the target. **Distribute** your **message** through **media**. **Disrupt** the **opposition**. Brand them as **toxic**. End their relationships.

Again, the path forward does not have to be conflict. The door is open for change. We can find a **win-win**. But if we have to play their **zero-sum game**, this is how we win.

CULTURE

Changing Culture

Culture is the set of default assumptions made in relationships.

For example, in Western society if I extend my hand and introduce myself at a public gathering, the default assumption is that you will shake hands with me. If someone refused to shake my hand, people would assume they had a strong animosity towards me and did not like me.

Monogamy is a default assumption in some cultures. Certain gender roles are a default assumption in some cultures. Eating meat is a default assumption in some cultures. You get the idea.

Changing culture means changing people's default assumptions.

In America, it used to be the default assumption that your male children would be circumcised. Now, it is a choice. The default assumption has changed from "you will circumcise" to "you will have to make the circumcision decision."

In Europe, there is no "circumcision decision." The default assumption is that you will keep your children intact. When we talk about "circumcising cultures," we are talking about what the default assumption is among a group of people.

This doesn't mean you can't do something different. People often form intentional communities where the default assumption is different from the rest of the world. However, these are known as "subcultures" because they are not the default among the dominant culture.

Cultural Assumptions

Cultural assumptions are not good or bad, except in how well they serve people's needs.

If you are in relationship with someone for a long time, you will develop certain cultural assumptions. For example, in the culture of my family, we hug when we say goodbye. I don't have to ask my family if they want a hug when I leave, because after years of knowing them, I know it's assumed.

If you had no assumptions in relationship, you would be starting from zero every time you saw someone. It would be hard to have a romantic relationship, if every time you saw your partner you had to re-explain your assumptions to them. Deep relationships require some assumptions.

When you enter relationship, you set those assumptions. For example, when you first started seeing someone, you might have had a conscious conversation with them saying that you wanted to be monogamous. Over time, that becomes an assumption. Your partner assumes that is still the case unless you have a conscious conversation asking to change that assumption.

Whereas relationship assumptions are consciously chosen, cultural ones are often not. I never had a conversation with the rest of the world where we agreed that shaking hands was the proper greeting. My family never had a conversation agreeing to say goodbye with a hug. Some cultural assumptions may even go back thousands of years.

For example, when someone sneezes, there is a cultural assumption in Western culture that someone will say "bless you." This assumption began in the Middle Ages, when people were dying of the Black Plague. Sneezing was a sign you might be getting sick, so people would bless you to make sure you didn't die from the plague.

Now, there is no longer any Black Plague, and we don't cure illnesses with Catholic blessings. Yet that cultural assumption continues so strongly that it seems a bit rude when you sneeze and someone doesn't say "bless you."

Cultural assumptions continue until they are questioned.

The cultural assumption to say "bless you" is mostly harmless. However, not all cultural assumptions are. Circumcision is obviously one such assumption.

When cultural assumptions make it impossible for people to meet their needs, especially in early childhood, they develop unmet needs that manifest as **toxic** behaviors. These needs can only be met by questioning cultural assumptions and changing culture.

How Culture Changes

What causes people to question their cultural assumptions?

People question assumptions for three reasons:

1) **It meets their needs.**

   Children are naturally curious and ask questions. People raised in a way that preserved their awareness will continue to ask questions in adulthood. That includes questions about their own actions and assumptions, which could be as simple as asking "what if" in the context of a thought experiment.

   However, most societies punish children for questioning cultural assumptions. There is a fear that questioning those assumptions will cause conflict within the tribe or social group. The simple need to explore and learn about the world is not enough for most people to question their assumptions in adulthood because it was not safe to do so in childhood.

   Most people do not question cultural assumptions until the pain of unmet needs is greater than the pain of change.

   For example, if someone comes from a fast food culture and

starts to experience health problems that will likely kill them, the pain of health issues might be greater than the pain of questioning assumptions about what they eat.

Likewise, people frequently question their culture due to emotional pain. If the dominant cultural assumptions include the idea that you will repress your feelings or sexual desires, the pain of those unmet needs might force you to question the cultural assumptions that prevent you from fulfilling them.

Although the pain of circumcision is significant, if someone is not aware of that pain, then the pain of questioning cultural assumptions might seem greater. Many question circumcision due to the pain of circumcision's consequences, or the pain of seeing a child go through it. Even the need to keep children safe can be a need that drives awakening around this issue.

2) **They are exposed to new assumptions.**

Someone might change their cultural assumptions when they are exposed to a different culture. Cultures frequently interact with each other and influence one another.

Culture shock occurs when someone visits a different culture and is forced to see cultural assumptions they didn't know they had. However, there is usually a second culture shock when they return home and see their previous cultural assumptions in the light of the culture they visited.

They might find they prefer one culture to another. They might bring their new culture with them, make a conscious choice to choose their former culture, or combine the two in some new way. However, whatever they chose is no longer an assumption, but a conscious choice.

Culture shock can occur on a smaller level, like someone from a small town culture visiting the big city for the first time, or someone from a small religious community spending time around non-believer friends. It could even occur in a relationship, when two people see another style of relationship that is different.

Being exposed to different assumptions forces us to question our own.

3) **They are forced to through relationship.**

If someone you are in relationship with demands you relate to them in a different way, it might force you to become aware of your assumptions and question them.

For example, if your default cultural assumption is that you will send your children to public school, and your spouse adamantly thinks they should be homeschooled, you may have to question your assumptions about schooling to maintain your relationship.

Even if someone makes an individual change in their cultural assumptions, they will eventually have to share those assumptions with those they are in relationship with.

People come to Intactivism through all three reasons.

They discover the issue due to their own curiosity, or due to the pain of circumcision. They are exposed to non-circumcising cultures, both abroad and next door among subcultures of friends who don't circumcise. Or, they are forced to confront the issue by a friend, colleague, or spouse who raises it.

Pain And Desire

When Intactivists talk about changing culture, they are trying to get people to question their assumptions and create new cultural assumptions. Values like personal freedom, bodily autonomy, and human rights are already cultural assumptions in most Western cultures.

It is possible for people to have conflicting cultural assumptions. The nature of most assumptions is that they are unexamined. If both circumcision and sexual freedom are unexamined assumptions that someone holds, they will not notice the contradiction between these values until awareness is brought to that contradiction and they are forced to question their assumptions.

Most people have shame around being "wrong." Needs that caused them to behave in ways their parents or caregivers did not like were shamed and punished. As a consequence, admitting a mistake or false belief often feels unsafe, especially if someone has identified with that belief and sees it as a part of themselves.

The need to feel right, look good, or belong is okay. These needs can be **aligned** when people realize that it is possible to do the right thing, look good, and belong *through* change. However, most people will not change until pain forces them too.

People change for two reasons: pain or desire.

For example, if you see an attractive person from a fitness subculture and desire to look like they do, you might change your assumed food and exercise habits. If your current diet is causing you the pain of health problems, you might also do the same.

Activists often use both.

When new parents research circumcision, they usually do so from the *desire* to do what is best for their children. This desire exposes them to new information, causing them to question their cultural assumptions.

When activist efforts remove circumcision from Medicare coverage, the *pain* of having to pay hundreds of dollars out of pocket for circumcision forces some parents to question their cultural assumptions.

All three of our above reasons people question cultural assumptions – needs, new assumptions, or relationship – can come from pain or desire.

Someone might have a need they pursue out of desire, or an unmet need causing them pain. They might see another culture and desire to be like it, or find the contrast of that culture painful. They might also desire relationship with someone who forces them to question their assumptions, or feel the pain of conflict with someone whose assumptions are different.

Both paths are legitimate.

The work of activism is to make the pain of unconsciousness greater than the pain of awareness, and to make people desire the change the activist wants.

The Risks Of Pain And Desire

When activists show images of babies bleeding during circumcision, they use the motivation of pain. When activists show images of happy intact babies, they use the motivation of desire.

Both methods can work. Both methods can fail.

The danger of using pain as a motivation is that people will associate the pain with you and believe you are the cause of it.

For example, if you yell at someone on the street, they might assume you are just causing them senseless pain and avoid you. If you approached them and made them feel good, they might have listened to what you have to say.

The danger of desire as a motivation is that people will not want what you offer badly enough to go through the pain of change.

How many times have you gently sent someone activist videos or literature, had them say they will "check it out," only to have them never get to it? They might have genuinely desired to read it, but not as much as they desired free time to spend on other things.

Desirable Culture

If Intactivists wish to change culture, they must become a culture that people desire.

The image of Intactivists often projected to the world is one of unhappiness. They are seen as "whiny" people focused on negative subjects and past pains.

In reality, many of the activists I've met are intelligent, happy people who want to better the world and protect children. They are incredibly giving, spend their free time helping others, and are exactly the kind of people anyone would want in their group or tribe.

On the flip side, circumcising groups often project an image of status and professionalism. They are seen as successful people going about the important work of the world.

In reality, many circumcising groups are full of fearful people, constantly worried they will lose membership in their group if they voice the stress and psychological pain they are under. Their relationships are transactional, and they cannot be fully honest with others or themselves.

When people accept a culture, they often do so wholesale.

For example, if I talk about the culture of veganism, what images do you imagine? The lingering cultural stereotype of vegan overlaps with what people might describe as "hippy" or "crunchy." Yet it is possible for suit-wearing Wall Street businessmen to be vegan. If someone desires the culture of Wall Street, they might think veganism is not for them – when the two cultures are actually compatible.

I began practicing Zen meditation as a teenager, because a guy who played in a punk band and worked on monster movies wrote about it. Had I learned about Zen from a stereotypical Zen priest, I might have thought it wasn't for me. Seeing someone who came from a culture I desired as a teenager describe how Zen improved his life made me also desire to try it.

Many worry that if they accept the message of Intactivism, they will also have to adopt other perceived cultural traits. They fear they will be perceived as low status, will need to become unhappy about their body, or will yell at opposition groups. For these people, high status, happiness, and freedom from conflict are legitimate needs that seem incompatible with Intactivism.

If activists wish to persuade these people to change, they must show that cutting culture is painful and that Intactivist culture is desirable.

For example, when was the last time you shared the message of how rewarding this work is? Or the positives this movement or issue has brought to your life?

Although becoming aware of this issue was initially painful, it has improved my life.

Becoming aware of circumcision allowed me to heal and integrate a lot of feelings I previously couldn't explain. It's made me more aware of my body and sexuality and better able to enjoy both those things. It's connected me to some of the most interesting people I've ever met and given me an opportunity to help others. Plus, when I have a family of my own, I will be better able to protect and love my own children and create a better future for them.

That is a lot more desirable than a culture where people are not accepted or loved unless they carve up children's genitals.

Improve Yourself

It is easier to project an image of desirable culture the more desirable your culture actually becomes. In other words, the more you improve your culture, the easier your activism will become.

When you work on yourself, you are actually helping the movement. When you heal your unmet needs, you are helping. When you improve your relationships, you are helping. When you become more successful, you are helping.

Your personal needs and growth can be aligned with the needs of the movement. You do not have to choose between your activism and a good life. You can have both and fulfill both needs at the same time.

The image you project matters.

Do you think people would be more likely to hear my message if I was broke, or a millionaire? If I was unable to maintain a relationship, or clearly could get the partners I desire? If I had constant public drama, or received praise from others?

It's the same message either way, but people want to be a part of a culture they desire.

Safe Culture

Desirable culture is different to different people.

The culture that people desire depends on their needs.

For example, one person might desire to be a part of a business culture because they want money. Another might avoid that culture because they feel they will not be accepted unless they conform to social standards that will not serve them.

People go towards whichever culture creates the safest relationship.

If people's needs are made safe and fulfilled by a culture, they will go towards that culture.

People avoid cultures they feel will shame or reject them. They go towards cultures that make their needs okay and fulfill those needs.

For example, someone who has a need for their sexuality to be accepted will avoid cultures that shame them for their sexuality and go towards cultures that accept them for their sexuality.

These cultures might have assumptions that have nothing to do with sexuality, yet people will accept those other assumptions in order to belong to the culture. For example, someone who joins a church culture might dress in a more conservative way, despite the fact it is possible to be religious and dress like a punk.

"**All your needs are okay**" is a practical strategy for creating safe culture. This does not mean that you need to tolerate **toxic** behavior, because **toxic** behavior is not safe. However, it does mean understanding and validating the underlying need.

Keep in mind: the opposition will attempt to make you appear **toxic**.

The opposite of **toxic** is *safe*.

Multiculturalism

Part of the challenge of creating safe culture is that Intactivism is a **coalition** of people coming from multiple cultures and subcultures.

The mere presence of some cultures might feel unsafe to other cultures.

For example, deeply religious people might find the presence of ardent atheists unsafe. People from one side of the political spectrum might find the presence of the opposite side unsafe. Feminists might find the presence of men's rights activists unsafe, or vice versa.

However, if we wish to reach the majority, we will need people from multiple cultures and subcultures. This means we need to find a way for multiple cultures to coexist safely.

This feeling that another culture is unsafe usually comes from assumptions about that culture and the belief that other cultures will behave in ways that make you unsafe.

For example, if you've heard that another culture hates or is bigoted towards people like you, you might fear that people from that culture will threaten your need for acceptance and make you unsafe if you are allowed into the movement.

Here we must question our own assumptions about other cultures. Are all people from their culture like that? Or has someone **toxically branded** them in an effort to win a different political conflict? Is the activist you disagree with actually treating you in **toxic** ways? Or is that just your assumption about how they will behave?

It is possible to find **alignment** around this issue with people you disagree with on other issues. Intactivists do not have to resolve every other political conflict to work together to protect children and end circumcision. We can treat each other in ways that are safe while holding different perspectives.

There is a difference between beliefs and actions. Just because you've heard a culture is toxic doesn't mean you have to become toxic towards them. Do not let someone else's bad beliefs cause you to take bad actions, or *you* will become the **toxic personality**.

The process by which you create **alignment** between cultures is the same process by which you create **alignment** within yourself and between individuals. The needs of a collective culture might be more complex, but they can be **aligned**.

For example, feminists need a world with gender equality where consent matters. Men's rights activists need a world in which men's needs matter and they are treated fairly. Both of these needs can be met by ending circumcision, so they are **aligned** around this issue.

If genuine **incompatibility** exists between you and an activist with different beliefs, you don't have to **collaborate**, but keep in mind: You will not end circumcision without **collaboration**.

That said, if someone is actually behaving in **toxic** ways, all the same rules about **toxic personalities** apply. This kind of **toxicity** has to do with behavior, not ideology.

When I hear people say that certain subcultures or belief systems should not be allowed in the Intactivist movement, I think of my parents.

My parents are fundamentalist evangelical Christians, who have both published articles with conservative political and religious perspectives. Most ideological requirements I've heard people propose as backing a shared desire to end circumcision would have excluded my parents.

When people propose ideological requirements, they are inadvertently saying that they would have denied my family the truth of Intactivism, and allowed me to be cut.

Do you think I deserve genital cutting?

Do you think proposing ideas that would lead to that outcome makes me feel safe?

Even if someone holds beliefs you disagree with, their children deserve safety and protection. Many people come to Intactivism from a belief system that is different from their parents'. If we wish to protect all children, then we cannot deny their parents our message over other ideological disagreements.

This goes both ways, of course. If people come to Intactivism from other cultures, they must **stay on message**, and create safe relationship with other activists. It is possible to expect people to act in **collaborative** ways while still allowing different perspectives.

Intactivist Culture

Every culture has assumptions, including subcultures.

Intactivism as a subculture is no different.

For example, one of the cultural assumptions of Intactivism is that "men's grief around circumcision is valid." If someone were to belittle a man for having grief over circumcision, they would be violating a cultural taboo in the subculture of Intactivism.

This is a healthy cultural assumption, because it serves the needs of people in the movement and creates safe relationship for people who have those needs.

However, not all assumptions are beneficial.

Many activists have a cultural assumption that money is bad, and that receiving money for activist work is not okay. Is this assumption healthy? Does it meet activist needs or bring us closer to the goal of ending circumcision?

The assumption that money is bad might serve other needs.

For example, activists who feel money is bad might not want relationships in the movement to become transactional or attract people who care more about money than the cause. They might want their work to be valued, whether or not they have money to contribute or can get money for their work. They might even have unmet needs that need healing in their own relationship to money.

All of these needs are okay. There are ways to meet and align those needs while making it okay for some activists to receive money for their work.

The process by which you change culture internally is the same as changing culture externally.

This is why I make it a point to **pace** potential needs in conflict with the need for money, validate them as okay, and then **lead** somewhere new.

Some of you will follow. Others won't. Maybe I missed the need or belief you needed me to **pace**. Maybe the idea that you could receive money for activist work is too big a **lead**. Maybe you just can't see how your needs would be **aligned** with that.

Part of the challenge of working through **media** is that you have to guess what your audience's assumptions will be. In mass **media**, you might have readers coming from wildly different assumptions.

However, I hope by now I've convinced you that you will not end circumcision without **resources** – one of which is **money** – and that it's okay to question cultural assumptions that do not meet our needs.

Activist Assumptions

What are the default assumptions of your activism?

Right now, "share the message" is the default assumption of Intactivist culture.

There is a cultural assumption within Intactivism that if we just "share the message" of Intactivism circumcision will end, and that focusing on that step alone is the best use of activist **resources**.

In this book, I question that assumption, and propose that ending circumcision will require activists to **recruit**, **organize**, and gather **resources**.

If I want to change the "share the message" assumption within our subculture, how could I do that?

Well, with the principles of this book.

In order to change the subculture of Intactivism, I **distributed** my **message** through **media** (this book, which you are reading now) to a **targeted** audience of **likely allies** already involved on this issue.

I **paced** the experiences, beliefs, and values of the movement. I showed the *pain* of the current "share the message" model and that the *desire* to end circumcision could be fulfilled through the organizer model.

Plus, by the end of this book, I plan to **recruit** you to a new **collaboration**, which will allow you to move from **messengers** to **organizers**. Keep reading through the epilogue.

There are other cultural ideas I'd like to promote, as well.

I'd like people to heal and **align** their needs. I'd like people to create safe relationships. I'd like people to **recruit** more **people** and **resources** into the movement. I'd like activists to **train** and constantly learn new **skills**. I'd like people to know that all of their needs are okay.

I think these are healthy cultural assumptions, because they fulfill our shared needs.

Continual Change

Changing culture is a continual process of improvement.

There is no endpoint at which your culture will be "done," because the needs of the people within that culture are continually changing. The cultural assumptions that served one group of people might not serve another.

However, there is an endpoint to this issue.

Ending circumcision.

Once you've followed this model, how do you win the endgame?

ENDGAME

Submitting The Opposition

There is a saying in Brazilian Jujitsu: *"position before submission."*

"Position before submission" means that before you can make your **opposition** submit, you must put them into a position in which you can do so.

Likewise, before we can end circumcision, we have to achieve a **position** in which we actually have the **resources** to change culture, win a lawsuit, or pass a law.

In this context, your **position** is how close you are to ending circumcision.

In this book, we've already laid out the whole path. Where are you on this map now?

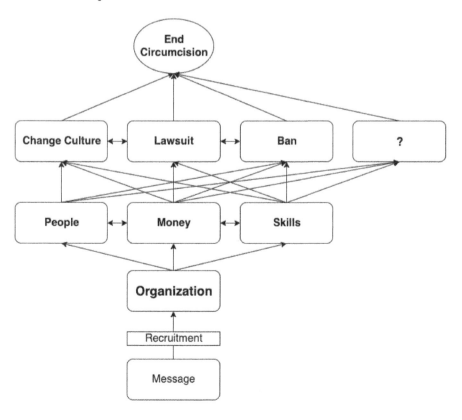

If you just "share the message," what is your position?

If you have multiple **organizations** with large amounts of **resources** that are actively **recruiting** and creating **targeted media** on a regular basis, what is your position?

Who is more likely to make the **opposition** submit and end circumcision?

Before you can reach the **endgame** of ending circumcision, you must get in position.

Building Your Position

Every action you take should better your position.

For example, by making my film, I'm in a better position than when I started.

Making my film positioned me to appear on podcasts. Each podcast I do better positions me by increasing my audience. Many of the podcasts I do have an audience of **likely allies**.

Having an audience within the Intactivist movement positioned me to write this book. This book also better positions me by allowing me to **train**, **recruit**, and **organize** more **skilled** people.

Activists who just "share the message" are constantly starting from zero. If you "share the message" with someone and they walk off without being **recruited**, you have to start all over with the next person. If that person was **recruited** into your **organization** and contributed **resources**, then your position would increase.

Right now, the **opposition** is very well positioned. Pro-circumcision **organizations** have significant **resources** and relationships with a broad **coalition** of **shared allies** and **neutral** institutions.

While it is possible to defeat **opposition** with less **resources**, it is easier the more you build your position.

Endgame Positions

Each **endgame** might require different positioning.

The **endgame** is any position that is one step away from ending circumcision.

In our current model, the **endgame** positions are change culture, win a lawsuit, pass a ban, or potential dark horse options.

Working backwards with our knowledge of the organizer model, we can see what position is required for each submission.

What would it take to ban circumcision?

You would need relationships with politicians. You would need **shared allies** in **organizations** that influence them. You would need to build a **coalition**. You need lots of **resources**. You might need to end **opposition** relationships with those politicians, since many will not go up against powerful opposition constituents.

What would it take to win a lawsuit?

You would need **skilled** lawyers. You need **money**. You would need enough people to find the right case or plaintiff. You might also need **skilled** researchers. You might also need enough of a political presence that you can prevent the **opposition** from reversing whatever win you achieve by passing a new law.

With both ban and lawsuit, you might need to change culture enough that voters, jury members, or judges are **likely allies** to your legal change, or at least close enough that they can be **paced** into your becoming **allies**.

What would it take to change culture?

You would need a lot of **messaging**, which could only be achieved through **media**. Creating media would require **resources, skilled** creators, and **media organizations** with high **distribution**.

You might need to **brand opposition organizations** as **toxic** to **shared allies** and **neutral** institutions in **media**, make sure the **opposition** does not brand you as **toxic**, and ensure you have a safe, desirable culture.

As you can see, each **endgame** might require slightly different positioning. For example, changing culture will require more people with **skills** in **media**. Winning a lawsuit will require more people with **skills** in law. Both require **money**.

However, from each list, you know what you still need to do. Focus on **recruiting** the **resources** (**people, money, skills**) needed for your chosen **endgame** position. Even if you discover a dark horse **endgame**, the same principles apply.

Playing The Long Game

Winning the game of Intactivism might require playing the long game.

There is an immediate gratification to "sharing the message." It feels good to express your beliefs and feelings, especially when there are unmet needs around having your pain seen.

However, winning the game of Intactivism might require work that furthers your position without being immediately gratifying.

Training in new **skills, recruiting** people who already agree with you, and creating safe relationships between existing **organizations**

might not give the same thrill as debating the **opposition**, but they bring us closer to the goal.

Right now, Intactivism feels challenging because activists do not have access to the **organization** and **resources** that exist on other issues. However, as activists who have been involved in this issue a long time will tell you: it is easier now than it used to be.

Intactivism is easier now because previous generations of activists have furthered our position. There are more **skilled** people working on this issue than ever before. More **people**. More **organizations**. More **allies**. More **media**.

It is easy to wish there were more **resources** available for this issue, but when the next group of activists looks at your work, how much more will you have furthered their position?

Whatever complaints you have about our current position, they will not change unless we solve them. There are a lot of **resources** in the world. Go **organize**, and **recruit**.

The Endgame Will Feel Easier

You will know you are in the endgame when things feel easier.

Right now, changing culture or passing a law might feel like distant goals. However, these goals will feel easier the closer we are to reaching them.

You will know you are in the **endgame** when vague ideas like "file a lawsuit" become clear plans like "connect this person in our **organization** with the **skilled** lawyer we **recruited**."

The reason European nations are more likely to end circumcision first is that they are better positioned. Europe already has a cultural assumption that children should be kept intact. The only assumption

European Intactivists need to question is, "Why don't we already have a law against this?" European activists also have more **shared allies** with greater access to **neutral** institutions.

Plus, opposition **organizations** are not as well positioned in Europe. There are fewer of them, and they have less **resources**.

Nevertheless, this is a global conflict. There are still ways for European activists to further their position. If European activists further their position, it will help American activists. If American activists change their culture, it will help Europe.

There is potential in Intactivism for worldwide **collaboration**.

There Is No "One Thing"

Many people are looking for the "one thing" that will end circumcision.

The one protest. The one message. The one event.

Many people thought my film would be the "one thing."

When I was making my film, one of my interview subjects showed me an issue of *The Saturday Evening Post* which featured graphic photos of circumcision. If you've seen my film, you've seen those photos. They are still used on protest images today.

He said a lot of people thought that publication would be the "one thing." People would see those images, and it'd be a breakthrough moment for the issue. It was barely a blip.

There is no "one thing" that will end circumcision.

When circumcision ends, it will be possible only because of hundreds of activists furthering the Intactivist position until we finally achieve that goal.

It will end because all of us **organize** and **collaborate** together.

Start Building Now

There is a dangerous valley between our current position and the **endgame**.

Right now, the **opposition** is inactive. They do not see Intactivists as a serious threat, because we lack **resources**. When the **opposition** sees Intactivists gathering **resources**, they might feel threatened and begin actively working against us.

Opposition groups have already shown how they might react during conflicts like the SF MGM ballot initiative to ban circumcision, or in conflicts with other movements like the anti-vaccination movement.

There might be a co-ordinated effort to brand Intactivism as **toxic**, destroy activist relationships, and build a **coalition** that uses **shared allies** to deny activists access to **neutral platforms**.

How well Intactivists handle this depends on how well we have prepared.

There is a saying among soldiers that "you don't rise to the occasion; you sink to the level of your training." Activists might think that in a political conflict they will suddenly have a breakthrough moment in which "all of the sheeple wake up." The more likely scenario is that activists fall back on default cultural assumptions and do whatever behavior feels the safest.

If they are **organized** and have **recruited resources**, they will be able to **collaborate** and **distribute** their **message**. However, it will be hard to build those relationships and **recruit** those **resources** under the pressure of attack.

How safe are your relationships? How **organized** are your **people**? What **allies** have you **recruited** to your **coalition**? What **skills** have you **trained**? What **resources** have you gathered?

Now is the time to build your position.

When the **opposition** tries to **disrupt** you, it will become harder.

Don't wait.

Start organizing now.

AFTERWARD:
INTACT MOVEMENT

Call To Action

Talk is easy.

Execution is hard.

It would be easy for me to just lay out a strategy.

However, the game is not "explain the strategy."

The game is **recruiting**.

This is the part where I **recruit** you.

Join IntactMovement.com.

Why I Created Intact Movement

My film *American Circumcision* was designed to solve a **message** problem.

Intact Movement is designed to solve an **organization** problem.

Prior to making *American Circumcision*, when people would ask about how they could learn about the circumcision issue, I'd rattle off a list of dozen books, YouTube videos, and websites they could check out.

The list was confusing. Many had good information, but varied in the quality of their presentation. Some were long academic books that most people would not read.

I wanted something simple, clear, and interesting that I could direct someone to that would give them a complete education on the issue.

Enter *American Circumcision*.

Now, when someone asks me about the issue of circumcision, I say, "watch *American Circumcision*."

Watching one good documentary is a lot easier an ask than reading a dozen academic books. Because the ask is clearer and simpler, more people watch my movie than my twelve book academic reading list.

After making *American Circumcision*, I got messages from people asking how they could get involved with the Intactivist movement. I'd rattle off a list of dozen organizations, and never hear from them again.

The list of organizations had the same problem. Many were great groups, but they were not always the right fit for the person contacting me. Without getting to know every stranger who emailed me, I had no way of knowing where the best use of their skills was or which organization needed them. Plus, emailing a dozen different groups was not an easy ask.

I wanted something simple, clear, and interesting that I could direct someone to so they could join an organization and take action.

Enter Intact Movement.

Now, when someone asks me how to get involved on this issue, I can say "join Intact Movement."

Intact Movement is an organizing hub for the Intactivist movement. It allows people to search activist organizations, find ones near them, contact them, communicate with other activists, collaborate, and get involved.

Intact Movement Differs From Social Media

Right now, most organizations do their organization through social media. This is dangerous, because these are neutral platforms that could change their rules at any point.

Social media creates the illusion of recruitment. Just because someone "liked" your page does not mean you will be able to contact and mobilize them.

Real organizing and recruitment would mean moving passive allies who "liked" your page into a system where you can contact them, ask for resources, and collaborate with them.

If the strength of our movement is the strength of our relationships, we do not want neutral intermediaries between those relationships, especially if opposition could act on those platforms with the intention of ending relationships.

Existing social media is designed to sell your attention to advertisers. Intact Movement is designed with the principles of this book in mind, to connect activists with each other for organization and collaboration. Many of our features are location based, and designed to lead you to real-world relationships with other activists based on shared goals, rather than endless scrolling.

Intact Movement is built for recruitment, organization, collaboration, and increasing the resources of the entire movement.

How To Recruit Using Intact Movement

One way to recruit someone is to just say:

"Join Intact Movement."

There, they will enter their contact information and be able to contact any organization.

If you already have an organization, you can say:

"Join Intact Movement, and follow our organization."

There, they will be able to see events your organization creates, find other members near them, see what skills your need for collaboration, or even directly contribute money through the site.

You can also create private forums visible only to selected members, for projects or discussions that require a select group.

How To Organize Using Intact Movement

Intact Movement might lead to new organizations.

Many people contact me from small towns asking what they can do. If I don't know anyone in their town, I can't help.

However, Intact Movement will allow them to search by location, find the other users in their area, and start a local organization.

Those activists might never find each other using existing social media, but they will be able to through our site.

This could also expand existing organizations by allowing them to form local chapters, contacting activists across the country who are looking to take action but haven't found a group yet.

Intact Movement Will Increase Collaboration

Right now, the Intactivist movement is scattered across platforms and organizations.

Each group has their own projects they are working on. Many organizations could better help one another but don't even know what the others are doing.

We will not win without collaboration.

Intact Movement will allow organizations to list the skills they are looking for and the projects supporters can collaborate on. Activists will be able to search those organizations and projects to see where their unique skills are needed.

Intact Movement will create collaborations that previously would have never happened, by allowing someone in the middle of nowhere to find that person halfway around the world who needs their skills.

Intact Movement Will Increase Resources

Every organization struggles with resources.

Right now, each Intactivist organization has their own donation method and store. Donating to multiple Intactivist groups requires tracking each down, finding their separate page, and using a new payment method for each one.

Intact Movement will allow organizations to raise money directly through our site and list their products to an audience of likely allies.

Activists will be able to find organizations' products more easily. If someone searches "info cards," they will be able to find a dozen different info cards from every organization, rather than having to compare across platforms.

We will be a platform where Intactivist organizations can increase their resources.

Intact Movement Is A Collaboration

Intact Movement will change as we learn what you need.

The version of the website that exists at the time I'm writing this will not be the version that exists when you read this book. We will be constantly iterating and improving.

When I say "join Intact Movement," I'm not saying this is the "one thing" that will end circumcision, or that I have it all figured out.

I'm inviting you to a collaboration.

We need your feedback to increase the strength of our platform.

As organizations use Intact Movement, we will discover what it needs to be. There may be things we learn through using the platform that completely change what features we include. This is a collaboration and a relationship as much as a product.

I'm not saying we can do everything. Web design is skilled labor, and we do not have the resources to execute every idea. However, we are here to serve you and your organization. If we can align with your needs, we will.

People have talked about doing something like this within the Intactivist movement for years. When I first got involved, it was the idea that someone should make a "Craigslist" for protest events. Later, it became a search function for different organizations.

When I approached some design firms with the idea, they told me it'd cost $50,000 for a fraction of what I wanted. I knew that even if I raised the money, it would be a transactional relationship that would make change expensive.

Then I found activists with skills to collaborate with. There were bumps in those relationships, but we have a version now, that will develop and grow based on what we learn as we use it.

With my film, I could do a lot as a lone operator. Intact Movement will require collaboration. It will only be as good as the people who use it.

Will you join me in collaboration?

Join here: **IntactMovement.com**

APPENDIX

Key Concepts

This page contains key concepts from each chapter. Use for reference.

Organize

- Gather resources (people, skills, money).
- You must organize.

Recruit

- Recruit active allies.
- Focus on neutrals and allies.

Message

- Target your message.
- Pace your audience's current beliefs.
- Use language they understand.

Media

- Distribution matters as much as message.
- Scale distribution through media.

Skills

- Increase your skill stack.
- You will not win without collaboration.

Needs

- All your needs are okay.
- The problem is needs in conflict.
- Align your needs.

Allies

- Align your allies.
- Avoid toxic personalities.
- Stay on message.

Opposition

- Toxic branding is messaging.
- Create safe relationships.
- Disrupt opposition.

Culture

- Culture is assumptions.
- Become desirable culture.
- Safe culture is desirable culture.

Endgame

- Position before submission.
- Play the long game.

The strength of our movement is the strength of our relationships.

<u>Key Concepts</u>

The Organizer Model

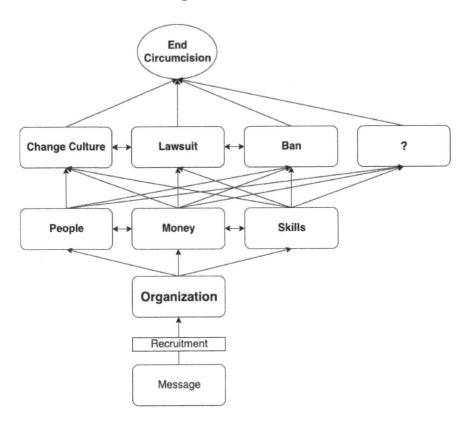

The Spectrum of Allies

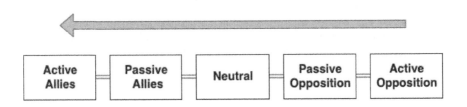

Glossary

Active allies: People and organizations actively working on your cause.

Active opposition: People and organizations actively working against your cause.

Align: To make it so your needs, or the needs of others, can be fulfilled by pursuing a common goal.

Alignment: When multiple needs or people can be fulfilled by pursuing the same goal.

Change culture: Shifting people's shared assumptions.

Collaboration: When people share skills and resources to work together on a common project.

Culture: Shared assumptions.

Deeper needs: Core desires or needs that drive a person's life.

Distribution: The way you share your message.

Disruption: When you destroy your opposition's ability to practice any step of the organizer model.

Easy-targets: People or organizations easily branded as toxic.

Endgame: Any position that is one point away from ending circumcision. Endgame positions include banning circumcision, large lawsuits, or changing culture.

Healing: Completely resolving an unmet need, often by having an opposite experience.

Hidden games: Games people secretly play to meet their unspoken deeper needs.

High-resource targets: People or organizations who bring a lot of resources into the movement.

Lead: A potential recruit.

Leading: When you say something your audience might not believe yet.

Likely allies: People, groups, or organizations who are currently **neutral** but are likely to become an **ally**.

Lone operator: A person working alone, without the benefit of organization.

Media: Messaging that reaches people even when you are not personally delivering the message.

Media organization: An organization with multiple people collaborating to create media.

Messaging: What you communicate to your audience.

Need: A thing someone desires or requires in order to survive or be fulfilled.

Neutrals: People who have not taken a side on your issue or are not aware of it.

Organization: Anything that allowed you to connect with and mobilize resources (people, money, skills).

Organizer model: A model of activism in which the goal is not just to "share the message" of your cause, but to target that message towards people you can recruit into organizations that will increase your resources.

Pace and lead: A persuasion tactic in which you mix statements your target audience already believes with new ideas they might not yet believe.

Pacing: When you say something your audience already believes is true.

Passive allies: People who support your cause but are not actively working on it.

Passive opposition: People who are against your cause but are not actively working against it.

Platform: A place where you distribute your message or media.

Pre-suasion: Any belief or concept that makes someone predisposed to accept a new idea they are not yet convinced of.

Recruitment: Bringing a lead into an organization where they can contribute resources.

Resources: People, skills, money. Anything that can be used to further you toward an endgame position.

Safe relationship: A relationship where all of a person's needs are okay.

Skill stack: A series of **skills** that are good in isolation but multiply exponentially when used together. Skills can all be held by one person or stacked through collaboration.

Skills: Any work that requires specialized knowledge or particular credentials.

Shadow need: A need or desire that even the person who wants it is not aware of.

"Share the message" model: A model of activism based on the idea that if you just "share the message" alone, eventually your cause will win.

Shared allies: People or organizations that are allies to more than one group.

Spectrum of allies: A model of social change that breaks people into five categories - actives allies, passive allies, neutral, passive opposition, active opposition - and suggests approaching each differently.

Target: The person, group, or organization you are trying to reach with your message.

Targeting: Trying to reach a particular person, group, or organization with your message.

Toxic: Relationship-ending qualities; the opposite of safe.

Toxic personality: Someone whose unconscious needs or hidden games work against your goals or the goals they claim to support.

Transactional relationship: A relationship that only continues as long as a transaction does.

Training: The process of learning new skills.

Win-win games: Games where both people or sides win together.

Win-win solutions: Solutions or outcomes where both sides get their needs met.

Zero-sum games: Games where one person or side wins, and the other loses.

Further Training

In this book, I suggest learning more about relationships, activism, and many other topics. Since you should always be training yourself in new skills, I've compiled a list of resources on my website in each of those areas and more.

If you're interested in developing new skills, go to my website here:

https://www.brendonmarotta.com/furthertraining

About the Author

Brendon Marotta is the director of the feature-length documentary *American Circumcision* and the founder of Intact Movement.